IMMACULATE

Library and Archives Canada Cataloguing in Publication

Cairney, John, 1968-, author
   Immaculate : a history of perfect innings in baseball / John Cairney.

Includes bibliographical references.
Issued in print and electronic formats.
ISBN 978-1-77161-115-2 (pbk.).--ISBN 978-1-77161-116-9 (html).--
ISBN 978-1-77161-117-6 (pdf)

   1. Baseball--United States--History. 2. Perfect games (Baseball).
3. Major League Baseball (Organization)--History. I. Title. II. Title: History
of perfect innings in baseball.

GV863.A1C362015   796.3570973   C2015-902610-5
                                              C2015-902611-3

Pubished by Mosaic Press, Oakville, Ontario, Canada, 2015.
Distributed in the United States by Bookmasters (www.bookmasters.com).
Distributed in the U.K. by Gazelle Book Services (www.gazellebookservices.co.uk).
MOSAIC PRESS, Publishers
Copyright © 2015 John Cairney

Printed and Bound in Canada.
Designed by Eric Normann

We acknowledge for their financial support of our publishing program
the Ontario Media Development Corporation

We acknowledge the financial sup-   Nous reconnaissons l'aide financière
port of the Government of Canada   du gouvernement du Canada par
through the Canada Book Fund   l'entremise du Fonds du livre du
(CBF) for this project.   Canada (FLC) pour ce projet.

 Canadian   Patrimoine
          Heritage   canadien

MOSAIC PRESS
1252 Speers Road, Units 1 & 2
Oakville, Ontario L6L 5N9
phone: (905) 825-2130

info@mosaic-press.com

www.mosaic-press.com

IMMACULATE

A History of Perfect Innings in Baseball

John Cairney

 mosaicPRESS

Acknowledgements

I wish to acknowledge several people in relation to this book. First, my brother Les Cairney who holds a special place in my heart and was on my mind often as I worked on this project. He was the first passionate sports fan I ever knew. Knowledgeable and articulate, he understood the potential for sport to ignite the imagination and ensnare the soul. He passed away some fifteen years ago and I was reminded of his absence many times during the course of writing this book. I would have loved the opportunity to discuss it with him, as we did so many times on so many different subjects. Despite his physical absence, my imagined conversations with him helped me greatly in completing this book. He is greatly missed by all whose lives he touched.

I would also like to acknowledge Matthew Goody, Editor at Mosaic Press. I am certain my proposal would not have made it very far had he not been a baseball fan. His editorial advice and content suggestions have made this a much better book than the original draft I submitted. Finally, a special thanks to my colleagues, students and staff at the INCH Lab at McMaster University—Christine, Matt, Heather, Tuyen, Emily, and Chloe. More than a bit surprised at the topic, they nevertheless assisted with editing and fact-checking. Any mistakes that remain are mine, not theirs.

To Monique, Logan, and Morgan. With all my love.

CONTENTS

INTRODUCTION

An Immaculate Feat of Pitching:
3 Batters, Nine Strikes, 3 Outs

An immaculate inning refers to a situation in which a pitcher, facing the first three batters in an inning, retires all three on consecutive strikes. In other words, three batters are retired on only nine pitches. It is the essence of mathematical balance: Three-nine-three. While simple in its expression, in practice it is anything but. In the recorded history of professional baseball, only seventy-three pitchers have achieved this feat, and only seventy-seven times. When one considers how many Major League pitchers since the late 1800s have played, let alone how many innings have been pitched since the beginning of professional baseball, pitching an immaculate inning is astonishingly rare.[1] And yet, it is not so astonishing as to garner the same

---

[1] It is harder to answer the question how rare it is than first appearances may suggest. For example, the number of teams and number of games played has varied over time. Moreover, not all games are nine innings—some finish in the middle of the ninth because the team batting first is behind and failed to score any runs rendering play in the bottom of the frame unnecessary. Some games are called early due to weather while others extend into extra innings. Moreover, some seasons are shorter than others owing to work stoppages. If overall, we restrict the time frame, to say, all games from the 2000 season onwards, and we ignore extra innings and games 8.5 innings or less (or rather, assume that all games, on average, are 9 innings long), then we can make a conservative estimate based on the following: 162 games per season, by 30 teams, by nine innings equals 43, 740 innings per year. Over fourteen seasons, that is 612,360 innings during regular season play (I am also ignoring post season play as only one immaculate inning

attention as pitching a perfect game, one of the rarest and most impressive achievements in all of baseball.[2]

There are many reasons why this may be so. To begin with, pitching an immaculate inning does not necessarily ensure victory in a game, whether that game is a regular season contest or game seven of the World Series; pitching a perfect game usually does (there are always exceptions, of course: Pedro Martínez and Harvey Haddix both saw perfect games evaporate in extra innings). Two, pitching a perfect game is a marathon achievement. The drama that unfolds is a direct result of the increasing realization of the improbability of the event. This places enormous pressure on the pitcher, the catcher, the rest of the players, and even the particularly superstitious fan who worries that even thinking a no-hitter is imminent will surely jinx it. It is not uncommon to hear pitchers and teammates utter the same sentiment after the fact.[3] Conversely, an immaculate inning is quick. Retiring three batters in a row on nine pitches could easily be missed by a bathroom break or a trip to the concession stand. More often than not, the realization that an immaculate inning has occurred comes the next day in the pages of the sport section, and only because the writer has bothered to go back over the boxscore and realize something really rare has just happened. Sometimes, there is no mention of it at all. It is perhaps not surprising that even in comprehensive baseball sources, such as Peter Morris's *A Game of Inches*, there is no mention of an immaculate inning, even though perfect games and no-hitters are part of that collection.[4] This is more observation than criticism. I do think that given the rarity of the feat however, more attention and recognition is deserved. That is the reason for this book. There has long been a fascination with the rare and the extraordinary in baseball. It has been the subject of many books and articles by both pundits and serious students of the game. This is not hard to understand.

as occurred during the playoffs). Since 2000, there have been 29 immaculate innings; if we divide 29 by 612,360, then the number of times it has occurred relative to the number of innings played is considerably small, .000047. Viewed this way, an immaculate inning is a very rare event indeed.

2 James Buckley Jr. *Perfect: The Inside Story of Baseball's Twenty Perfect Games.* Triumph Books, Chicago.

3 Buckley Jr., Ibid.

4 Peter Morris, *A Game of Inches: The story behind the innovations that shaped baseball.* Ivan R Dee, Chicago, 2010.

In a game where greatness is achieved by being able to consistently hit the ball three times out of ten; where the very nature of the game defies consistency and makes perfection seem like a hopeless quixotic quest; perfect execution, when it does occur, is cause for celebration. It keeps us coming back to the park. It is part of the beauty of the game. This book is a celebration of the pitchers who achieved perfection, if only for a brief moment in time.

Where does the term immaculate inning come from? It is not clear who first coined (or penned) the phrase, but beyond the more common linking of immaculate to conception in religion, the word simply means perfect or free from mistakes. A nine-pitch, three-strike inning is obviously perfect execution for a pitcher. It is probably true, however, that because perfect was already used in conjunction with pitching (a perfect game which occurs when there are no hits, walks or bases given on error), the synonym "immaculate" became the preferred way to describe when the side in an inning is retired on nine strikes.[5]

Aside from the name, what we can be certain of is summarized in the table below. It shows the names of all seventy-three pitchers who achieved this feat, at least to the time of the writing of this book. In the pages that follow, I will provide greater detail on each immaculate inning. There are, however, a few observations that can be made by just studying the list. For example, National League pitchers have pitched more immaculate innings than American League pitchers (46 versus 28).[6] Right-handed pitchers outnumber lefties more than three to one (56 versus 17). There have only been two recorded instances (so far) of an immaculate inning occurring after the 9th inning—Sloppy Thurston's perfect 12th; and Juan Pérez's 10th inning. To date, only one perfect inning has been pitched during the post-season. Only four pitchers have accomplished this feat more than once (Lefty Grove; Sandy Koufax; Nolan Ryan; Randy Johnson). Of the twenty-three pitchers on this list who are eligible for election to the Baseball Hall of Fame, less than half (nine in fact) are members.

---

5 http://www.sportingcharts.com/dictionary/mlb/immaculate-inning.aspx. Retrieved on August 3rd, 2013.

6 Nolan Ryan pitched for both leagues, and recorded an immaculate inning in both, so I have included him in both groups.

Table 1. Immaculate innings pitched, 1889-2014

	Date	Pitcher	Lefty / Righty	Team	Opposing Team	Batters Faced (in Order)	Inning
1	Jun 4 1889	John Clarkson	R	Boston Beaneaters (NL)	Philadelphia Quakers	1. Jim Fogarty 2. Sam Thompson 3. Sid Farrar	3rd
2	Jul 1 1902	Rube Waddell	L	Philadelphia Athletics (AL)	Baltimore Orioles	1. Billy Gilbert 2. Harry Howell 3. Jack Cronin	3rd
3	Oct 5 1914	Pat Ragan	R	Brooklyn Dodgers (NL)	Boston Robins	1. Possum Whitted 2. Butch Schmidt 3. Red Smith	8th
4	Sep 8 1921	Joe Oeschger	R	Boston Braves (NL)	Philadelphia Athletics	1. Bevo LeBourveau 2. Cy Williams 3. Ed Konetchy	4th
5	Aug 22 1923	Sloppy Thurston	R	Chicago White Sox (AL)	Philadelphia Athletics	1. Beauty McGowan 2. Chick Galloway 3. Sammy Hale	12th
6	Sep 24 1924	Dazzy Vance	R	Brooklyn Dodgers (NL)	Chicago Cubs	1. Sam Bohne 2. Bubbles Hargrave 3. Eppa Rixey	2nd
7	Aug 23 1928	Lefty Grove	L	Philadelphia Athletics (AL)	Cleveland Indians	1. Ed Morgan 2. Luther Harvel 3. Martin Autry	2nd
8	Sep 27 1928	Lefty Grove	L	Philadelphia Athletics (AL)	Chicago White Sox	1. Moe Berg 2. Tommy Thomas 3. Johnny Mostil	7th
9	Sep 7 1953	Billy Hoeft	L	Detroit Tigers (AL)	Chicago White Sox	1. Jim Rivera 2. Mike Fornieles 3. Chico Carrasquel	7th
10	Apr 17 1956	Robin Roberts	R	Philadelphia Phillies (NL)	Brooklyn Dodgers	1. Carl Furillo 2. Charlie Neal 3. Sandy Amorós	6th
11	Aug 2 1959	Jim Bunning	R	Detroit Tigers (AL)	Boston Red Sox	1. Sammy White 2. Jim Mahoney 3. Ike Delock	9th
12	Jun 30 1962	Sandy Koufax	L	Los Angeles Dodgers (NL)	New York Mets	1. Richie Ashburn 2. Rod Kanehl 3. Félix Mantilla	1st

Date	Pitcher	Lefty / Righty	Team	Opposing Team	Batters Faced (in Order)	Inning
13	Apr 19 1963 Sandy Koufax	L	Los Angeles Dodgers (NL)	Houston Colt .45s	1. Bob Aspromonte 2. Jim Campbell 3. Turk Farrell	5th
14	Jun 15 1963 Tony Cloninger	R	Milwaukee Braves (NL)	Philadelphia Phillies	1. Tony González 2. Clay Dalrymple 3. Rubén Amaro	8th
15	Apr 18 1964 Sandy Koufax	L	Los Angeles Dodgers (NL)	Cincinnati Reds	1. Leo Cárdenas 2. Johnny Edwards 3. Jim Maloney	3rd
16	Apr 19 1964 Bob Bruce	R	Houston Colt .45s (NL)	St. Louis Cardinals	1. Bill White 2. Charlie James 3. Ken Boyer	8th
17	Aug 11 1967 Al Downing	L	New York Yankees (AL)	Cleveland Indians	1. Tony Horton 2. Don Demeter 3. Duke Sims	2nd
18	Apr 19 1968 Nolan Ryan	R	New York Mets (NL)	Los Angeles Dodgers	1. Claude Osteen 2. Wes Parker 3. Zoilo Versalles	3rd
19	May 12 1969 Bob Gibson	R	St. Louis Cardinals (NL)	Los Angeles Dodgers	1. Len Gabrielson 2. Paul Popovich 3. John Miller	7th
20	Jul 6 1971 Bill Wilson	R	Philadelphia Phillies (NL)	Atlanta Braves	1. Darrell Evans 2. Hal King 3. Earl Williams	8th
21	Jul 10 1971 John Strohmayer	R	Montreal Expos (NL)	Philadelphia Phillies	1. Mike Ryan 2. Woodie Fryman 3. Denny Doyle	5th
22	Sep 24 1971 Milt Pappas	R	Chicago Cubs (NL)	Philadelphia Phillies	1. Greg Luzinski 2. Don Money 3. Mike Anderson	4th
23	Jul 9 1972 Nolan Ryan	R	California Angels (AL)	Boston Red Sox	1. Carlton Fisk 2. Bob Burda 3. Juan Beníquez	2nd
24	Sep 8 1977 Bruce Sutter	R	Chicago Cubs (NL)	Montreal Expos	1. Ellis Valentine 2. Gary Carter 3. Larry Parrish	9th

	Date	Pitcher	Lefty / Righty	Team	Opposing Team	Batters Faced (in Order)	Inning
25	Jun 23 1979	Pedro Borbón	R	Cincinnati Reds (NL)	San Francisco Giants	1. Mike Sadek 2. Gary Lavelle 3. Billy North	9th
26	Aug 25 1979	Lynn McGlothen	R	Chicago Cubs (NL)	San Francisco Giants	1. Larry Herndon 2. Joe Strain 3. Jack Clark	3rd
27	Sep 11 1979	Joey McLaughlin	R	Atlanta Braves (NL)	San Francisco Giants	1. Larry Herndon 2. Greg Johnston 3. Johnnie LeMaster	7th
28	Aug 7 1984	Ron Guidry	L	New York Yankees (AL)	Chicago White Sox	1. Carlton Fisk 2. Tom Paciorek 3. Greg Luzinski	9th
29	Oct 24 1985	Danny Jackson	L	Kansas City Royals (AL)	St. Louis Cardinals	1. Terry Pendleton 2. Tom Nieto 3. Brian Harper	7th
30	Sep 7 1987	Jeff Robinson	R	Pittsburgh Pirates (NL)	Chicago Cubs	1. Leon Durham 2. Andre Dawson 3. Rafael Palmeiro	8th
31	Jun 4 1989	Rob Dibble	R	Cincinnati Reds (NL)	San Diego Padres	1. Carmelo Martinez 2. Mark Parent 3. Garry Templeton	8th
32	Apr 29 1990	Jeff Montgomery	R	Kansas City Royals (AL)	Texas Rangers	1. Pete Incaviglia 2. Geno Petralli 3. Thad Bosley	8th
33	Jun 15 1991	Andy Ashby	R	Philadelphia Phillies (NL)	Cincinnati Reds	1. Hal Morris 2. Todd Benzinger 3. Jeff Reed	4th
34	Aug 30 1991	David Cone	R	New York Mets (NL)	Cincinnati Reds	1. Herm Winningham 2. Randy Myers 3. Mariano Duncan	5th
35	Sep 6 1991	Pete Harnisch	R	Houston Astros (NL)	Philadelphia Phillies	1. Wes Chamberlain 2. Dickie Thon 3. José de Jesús	7th
36	Jun 7 1992	Trevor Wilson	L	San Francisco Giants (NL)	Houston Astros	1. Jeff Bagwell 2. Eric Anthony 3. Rafael Ramírez	9th

	Date	Pitcher	Lefty / Righty	Team	Opposing Team	Batters Faced (in Order)	Inning
37	May 11 1994	Mel Rojas	R	Montreal Expos (NL)	New York Mets	1. David Segui 2. Todd Hundley 3. Jeff McKnight	9th
38	Aug 6 1994	Stan Belinda	R	Kansas City Royal (AL)	Seattle Mariners	1. Eric Anthony 2. Chris Howard 3. Luis Sojo	9th
39	Aug 13 1995	Todd Worrell	R	Los Angeles Dodgers (NL)	Pittsburgh Pirates	1. Mark Johnson 2. Angelo Encarnación 3. Steve Pegues	9th
40	Aug 22 1997	Mike Magnante	L	Houston Astros (NL)	Colorado Rockies	1. Ellis Burks 2. Harvey Pulliam 3. Jeff Reed	9th
41	Sep 18 1997	Roger Clemens	R	Toronto Blue Jays (AL)	Boston Red Sox	1. Nomar Garciaparra 2. John Valentin 3. Mo Vaughn	1st
42	Sep 23 1997	Doug Jones	R	Milwaukee Brewers (AL)	Kansas City Royals	1. Johnny Damon 2. Scott Cooper 3. Rod Myers	9th
43	Apr 14 1998	Jimmy Key	L	Baltimore Orioles (AL)	Chicago White Sox	1. Robin Ventura 2. Magglio Ordóñez 3. Ray Durham	2nd
44	May 9 1998	Mike Mussina	R	Baltimore Orioles (AL)	Tampa Bay Rays	1. Fred McGriff 2. Paul Sorrento 3. Rich Butler	9th
45	Jun 16 1998	Orel Hershiser	R	San Francisco Giants (NL)	Colorado Rockies	1. Eillis Burks 2. Vinny Castilla 3. Todd Helton	4th
46	Sep 2 1998	Randy Johnson	L	Houston Astros (NL)	Altanta Braves	1. Javy Lopez 2. Andruw Jones 3. Greg Colbrunn	6th
47	Sep 13 1998	Jesús Sánchez	L	Florida Marlins (NL)	Atlanta Braves	1. Tony Graffanino 2. Greg Maddux 3. Walt Weiss	3rd
48	Jul 15 1999	Shane Reynolds	R	Houston Astros (NL)	Detroit Tigers	1. Juan Encarnación 2. Brad Ausmus 3. Bobby Higginson	1st

	Date	Pitcher	Lefty / Righty	Team	Opposing Team	Batters Faced (in Order)	Inning
49	Sep 5 1999	B.J. Ryan	L	Baltimore Orioles (AL)	Cleveland Indians	1. Manny Ramirez 2. Jim Thome 3. Richie Sexson	6th
50	Apr 4 2000	Ugueth Urbina	R	Montreal Expos (NL)	Los Angeles Dodgers	1. F.P. Santangelo 2. Devon White 3. Mark Grudzielanek	9th
51	Aug 23 2001	Randy Johnson	L	Arizona Diamondbacks (NL)	Pittsburgh Pirates	1. Tony McKnight 2. Gary Matthews 3. Jack Wilson	6th
52	Apr 13 2002	Jason Isringhausen	R	St Louis Cardinals (NL)	Houston Astros	1. Daryle Ward 2. José Vizcaíno 3. Julio Lugo	9th
53	May 11 2002	Byung-Hyun Kim	R	Arizona Diamondbacks (NL)	Philadelphia Phillies	1. Scott Rolen 2. Mike Lieberthal 3. Pat Burrell	8th
54	May 18 2002	Pedro Martínez	R	Boston Red Sox (AL)	Seattle Mariners	1. Ichiro Suzuki 2. Mark McLemore 3. Rubén Sierra	1st
55	Jun 12 2002	Brian Lawrence	R	San Diego Padres (NL)	Baltimore Orioles	1. Brook Fordyce 2. Jerry Hairston, Jr. 3. Melvin Mora	3rd
56	Apr 15 2004	Brandon Backe	R	Houston Astros (NL)	Milwaukee Brewers	1. Bill Hall 2. Scott Podsednik 3. Craig Counsell	8th
57	Jun 13 2004	Ben Sheets	R	Milwaukee Brewers (NL)	Houston Astros	1. Pete Munro 2. Craig Biggio 3. José Vizcaíno	3rd
58	Sep 11 2004	LaTroy Hawkins	R	Chicago Cubs (NL)	Florida Marlins	1. Jeff Conine 2. Juan Encarnación 3. Álex González	9th
59	Jun 20 2006	Rick Helling	R	Milwaukee Brewers (NL)	Detroit Tigers	1. Curtis Granderson 2. Plácido Polanco 3. Iván Rodriguez	1st
60	Jul 6 2007	Buddy Carlyle	R	Atlanta Braves (NL)	San Diego Padres	1. Khalil Greene 2. Russell Branyan 3. José Cruz Jr.	4th

	Date	Pitcher	Lefty / Righty	Team	Opposing Team	Batters Faced (in Order)	Inning
61	Jun 8 2008	Rich Harden	R	Oakland Athletics (AL)	Anaheim Angels	1. Maicer Izturis 2. Howie Kendrick 3. Garret Anderson	1st
62	Jun 17 2008	Félix Hernández	R	Seattle Mariners (AL)	Florida Marlins	1. Jeremy Hermida 2. Jorge Cantú 3. Mike Jacobs	4th
63	Jun 20 2009	A.J. Burnett	R	New York Yankees (AL)	Florida Marlins	1. Josh Johnson 2. Chris Coghlan 3. Emilio Bonifacio	3rd
64	Sep 5 2009	Ross Ohlendorf	R	Pittsburgh Pirates (NL)	St. Louis Cardinals	1. Khalil Greene 2. Julio Lugo 3. Jason LaRue	7th
65	Aug 23 2010	Rafael Soriano	R	Tampa Bay Rays (AL)	Los Angeles Angels	1. Erick Aybar 2. Mike Napoli 3. Peter Bourjos	9th
66	May 6 2011	Jordan Zimmermann	R	Washington Nationals (NL)	Florida Marlins	1. Giancarlo Stanton 2. Greg Dobbs 3. John Buck	2nd
67	Jul 8 2011	Juan Pérez	L	Philadelphia Phillies (NL)	Atlanta Braves	1. Jason Heyward 2. Nate McLouth 3. Wilkin Ramírez	10th
68	Aug 16 2012	Clay Buchholz	R	Boston Red Sox (AL)	Baltimore Orioles	1. Adam Jones 2. Matt Wieters 3. Chris Davis	6th
69	Oct 1 2012	Wade Miley	L	Arizona Diamondbacks (NL)	Colorado Rockies	1. Jonathan Herrera 2. Drew Pomeranz 3. Josh Rutledge	3rd
70	May 29 2013	Iván Nova	R	New York Yankees (AL)	New York Mets	1. Ike Davis 2. Mike Baxter 3. Rubén Tejada	8th
71	Jul 30 2013	Steve Delabar	R	Toronto Blue Jays (AL)	Oakland Athletics	1. Adam Rosales 2. Coco Crisp 3. Chris Young	8th
72	May 8 2014	Brad Boxberger	R	Tampa Bay Rays (AL)	Baltimore Orioles	1. Steve Pearce 2. Jonathan Schoop 3. Caleb Joseph	6th

	Date	Pitcher	Lefty / Righty	Team	Opposing Team	Batters Faced (in Order)	Inning
73	May 17 2014	Cole Hamels	L	Philadelphia Phillies (NL)	Cincinnati Reds	1. Zack Cozart 2. Brandon Phillips 3. Todd Frazier	3rd
74	Jun 2 2014	Justin Masterson	R	Cleveland Indians (AL)	Boston Red Sox	1. Jonny Gomes 2. Grady Sizemore 3. Stephen Drew	4th
75	Jun 4 2014	Garrett Richards	R	Los Angeles Angels (AL)	Houston Astros	1. Jon Singleton 2. Matt Dominguez 3. Chris Carter	2nd
76	Jun 14 2014	Rex Brothers	L	Colorado Rockies (NL)	San Francisco	1. Michael Morse 2. Brandon Crawford 3. Gregor Blanco	8th
77	Jul 11 2014	Carlos Contreras	R	Cincinnati Reds (NL)	Pittsburgh Pirates	1. Jordy Mercer 2. Jeff Locke 3. Gregory Polanco	7th
78	Sep 17 2014	Brandon McCarthy	R	New York Yankees (AL)	Tampa Bay Rays	1. Wil Myers 2. Nick Franklin 3. Matt Joyce	7th

While these facts describe specific aspects of immaculate innings, they only hint at why they occur in the first place and they tell us nothing about if, or why, perfect innings have changed over time. Therefore, to begin to answer these questions, I have graphed where and how often an immaculate inning has occurred, and compared that against another rare feat, the perfect game (see Figure 1).

The first thing that stands out in this graph is that the overall trend for both events is similar: over time, the occurrence of both has generally increased. However, the occurrence of immaculate innings has risen more dramatically relative to perfect games, especially in the last thirty years. There is also a curious, shared period of time (1930s and 40s) when no perfect games or immaculate innings occurred. If we focus just on the trend line for immaculate innings, there are some other interesting things to note. First, the line is punctuated by three prominent spikes: the first occurs during the 1920s, the second during the 1960s, and then again in the 2000s. This means that there are specific periods in time where there are sharp increases in the number of immaculate innings pitched. Why this is so we can only guess, but here are some interesting possibilities.

During the first spike in the 1920s, two of the three pitchers to achieve the feat went on to be Hall of Famers—Dazzy Vance and Lefty Grove.

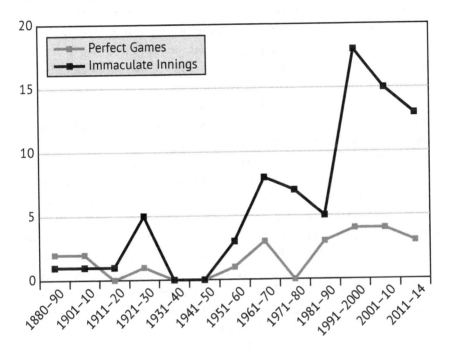

Figure 1.
The number of immaculate innings and perfect games pitched from 1889 to 2014

Grove actually recorded back-to-back immaculate innings (the only pitcher to do this) in just over a month. In the 1960s, the time of the second spike, four of the six pitchers that decade are also Hall of Famers— Sandy Koufax, who became the second pitcher to pitch two immaculate innings consecutively (though not back-to-back), Nolan Ryan (the third to pitch more than one perfect inning) and Bob Gibson. It remains to be seen if this trend will also define the most recent peak. Certainly Randy Johnson and Pedro Martínez are legitimate contenders for the Hall, both of whom recorded immaculate innings during that last spike period in the 2000s (Randy Johnson by the way, also pitched two immaculate innings, becoming the fourth pitcher to do so in history). In other words, there is at least some evidence for the claim that great innings come from the arms of great pitchers. There clearly appears to be an increase in the occurrence of this event during the periods when these great pitchers played the game.

What else can we make of these trends? It is interesting that two of these three time periods—the 1920s and the period from 2000s—are also known for facets (and controversies) of the game other than pitching. Stephen J. Gould has examined batting averages in professional baseball overtime since the turn of the 20th of century.[7] He was interested in trying to explain the disappearance of the .400 hitter. His analysis showed that beginning in 1920, league batting averages rose significantly, into the .270s-.280s, and remained this high until the 1940s. He described the transition from the early 1900s to 20's this way: "Scrappy, one run, slap-hit, grab-a-base-at-a-time play retreated and home run power became the name of the game."[8] This was the era of Babe Ruth. Flash forward to the early part of the 21st century; this too was an era of big hitters (Sammy Sosa, Barry Bonds etc.). The incredible power hitting numbers during this period is now referred to as the "steroid era" in modern baseball. What does all this have to do with immaculate innings? Perhaps nothing at all, but it is reasonable to speculate that the sharp increases in perfect innings pitched during these eras are not merely coincidence. After all, if batters are "swinging for the fences," then strikes and strikeouts will increase commensurately. A high swing and miss ratio, if only slightly, increases the likelihood that successive strikes and strikeouts will occur. Steroid use will certainly affect power, speed, and confidence, but likely not vision.[9] So there is no reason to assume that batters during this time were seeing the ball any better—just hitting harder, faster and therefore further. Of course, steroid use among pitchers may also have contributed to a spike in perfect innings at that same time juiced batters were piling up home runs. While these explanations might account for spikes and dips in the occurrence of perfect innings over time, they do not explain the overall increase in the number of immaculate innings that has occurred from 1889 to the present. This is more likely attributable to two, interrelated changes in the game: the expanded season has increased opportunities for more perfect innings and pitching has become increas-

7 Stephen J. Gould, "Losing the Edge" in *The Flamingo's Smile: Reflections in Natural History*, W.W. Norton, 1987, pp. 215-229.

8 Stephen J. Gould "Introduction" in Eliot Asinof, *Eight Men Out: the Black Sox and the 1919 World Series* Holt Paperbacks, 2000, p. xvii.

9 Lee Jenkins, "Baseball: Taking a Swing With Steroids," *New York Times* (June 6, 2004): http://www.nytimes.com/2004/06/14/sports/baseball-taking-a-swing-with-steroids.html?pagewanted=all&src=pm. Retrieved on Nov. 8th, 2013.

ingly specialized in the modern era. Today, pitching staffs have expanded dramatically to include starters, middle relievers, and closers. The latter are often called in to pitch one inning or even face a single batter (for specific lefty-righty matchups for example). Compare this to baseball in the late 1800s through to the first seventy or so years of the 20th century. For much of this time, teams relied on a small number of pitchers and these pitchers were expected to pitch the whole game unless they had to be taken out due to bad performance or injury. While relievers have existed since before 1900, they were not in widespread use until the 1970s, at which point nearly all teams had not only relief pitchers but closers too. Today five-man starting rotations are used by all teams in the league and there are between eleven and twelve pitchers on every team roster. Prior to the 1970s, teams might have one or two starting pitchers, pitching on short rest periods. Any fan, coach, manager or sports journalist will tell you that in today's game, you can't have enough pitching. With fewer pitches to pitch per game (and more rest between games), the starting pitcher does not have to worry about holding back to last all nine innings. When you consider this along with the fact that professional ballplayers are getting bigger and stronger thanks to both selective recruitment and better training, there is a perfect storm for increased immaculate innings. But these are not the only changes the game as seen. As I write this chapter, there is increased chatter in the media about defensive alignments, and whether baseball's new commissioner—Rob Manfred—should considering banning the shift (moving the infielders sometimes way out of position based on a batters tendencies to hit to one side of the field) altogether.[10] The concern, of course, is the decline in offense; specifically, runs per game, which has steadily declined over the past ten years. While some have argued the drop in run production to be due to defensive shifts, the numbers simply do not support that conclusion.[11] What is clear is that strikeouts have certainly increased at the same time run production has dropped. Power hitting and better pitching account for the drop in runs per game more than creative deployment of

---

10 Ben Lindbergh, "Banning New MLB Commissioner Rob Manfred's Proposed Ban on the Shift," Grantland.com, (January 26th, 2015): http://grantland.com/the-triangle/mlb-commissioner-rob-manfred-proposes-defensive-shift-ban/. Retrieved on April 1st, 2015.

11 Ted Berg, "Outlawing MLB's aggressive infield shifts makes no sense," *USA Today Sports*, (July 24th, 2014): http://ftw.usatoday.com/2014/07/mlb-infield-shifts-illegal-defense. Retrieved on April 1st, 2015.

players around the diamond. Therefore, the shift is probably not the cause for the increase in immaculate innings either.

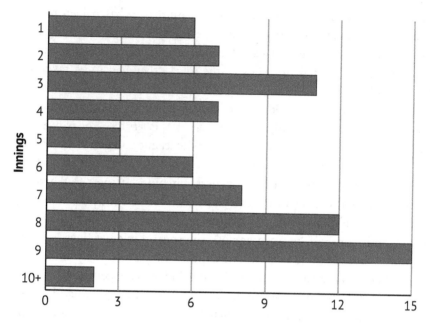

Figure 2.
Number of Immaculate Innings by What Inning it Occurred

While it makes sense that specialization and larger pitching rosters may be driving up perfectly pitched innings, do we have any evidence for these two explanations? Figure 2 shows the number of times three batters have been retired on nine pitches by inning. Although it looks like immaculate innings are somewhat more likely to occur in the 8th or 9th, (about 36% of the time), over the history of the game, 74% of the time perfect innings happened before the 8th. We can take this analysis even further to look specifically at the association between when an immaculate inning is pitched in a game (the inning in which it occurs) and the year in which it happened. After all, we know the 1970s really marked the modern day use of relievers and closers on a widespread basis throughout both leagues. If the institution of these new positions has actually increased the number of immaculate innings, we would expect to see more perfect innings occurring later in games after 1970 than before (something we cannot tell from just looking at Figure 2 alone). Below is a graph showing the years immaculate innings have occurred (1889 to 2014) by the inning in which the immaculate feat occurred.

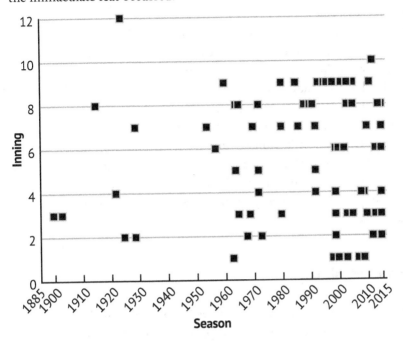

Figure 3.
Relationship between season and the inning in which an immaculate inning occurred

You don't have to be a sabermetrician to interpret what is happening in this picture: there is no discernible pattern in these data. Regardless of time, perfect innings occurred at virtually any point during a game. Statisticians summarize the relationship between two things (in this case year and the inning in which a perfect inning occurred) using a statistic called the correlation coefficient. The number it produces can range in value from 0 (which means the two things are completely unrelated) to 1.0 (which indicates a perfect association). The correlation coefficient for time and the inning in which perfection occurred is .049—in other words, very near 0. There is no association between year and when an immaculate inning occurred in a game. But before we put this particular explanation to rest, it is important to consider that increased specialization in pitching may not just affect situations in late game innings. Starters, knowing that they are on strict pitch counts, may throw harder earlier in the game. In other words, specialization spans the entire nine-inning game and this may be one reason why there is no clear pattern as to when a perfect inning occurs during a game.

There is one explanation though we cannot entirely dismiss when looking at these numbers: the overall increase in immaculate innings pitched does support the increased length of season explanation. Prior to 1919, the season for both leagues was 140 games. By 1962, that had increased to 162 (ignoring some variation owing to player strikes etc.). Looking again at Figure 1, it is apparent the rise in number of perfect innings occurs post-1962. However, it is unlikely that longer seasons are the sole reason immaculate innings have increased over time. As noted above already, increasing skill level, better conditioning and bigger, stronger players cannot be ignored entirely as part of the reason why immaculate innings appear to have increased.

The Focus of this Book

Examining statistics and trends is interesting but they provide an incomplete story. Who were the men who pitched these immaculate innings? What do we know about the events in question? Narratives, in addition to the numbers, are the compelling stories of baseball and are part of both the history and mythology of the game. They are as essential to the game as the numbers. While we know Abner Doubleday did not invent baseball one sunny day in Cooperstown, New York, the narrative, both the creation mythology and the story of the men who constructed it, are inextricably part of the game's history. We cannot neatly separate fact from fiction in this game—narrative reminds us of that, while numbers reinforce our desire to make it objective. In this book, I look at both numbers and stories. The sections that follow piece together a chronological record of immaculate innings that focuses on the pitchers who have achieved them. To make for an interesting read, I have consciously attempted to try not to be formulaic about the organization of these stories. Regardless, the histories of some pitchers are scant, and details of the actual innings themselves, especially those that occurred in the 19th and early to mid-20th century, are sparse. It is difficult to achieve uniformity in presentation given the information available. Whenever possible, I have tried to put a human face on the record by considering the pitchers biography, the time in which he lived and played, along with other achievements that may have been part of their career or personal life. When there were interesting stories about things that happened outside the game to these men—sometimes celebratory, sometimes tragic—I included these as well. Other times, I made connections to broader events in history and in popular culture when I felt it made sense. I make no claim, however, that these are comprehensive biographies. Many of the pitchers in this collection are already the subjects of comprehensive published biographies, which should be read in their own right. An immaculate inning is short, so it is fitting to chronicle them in a concise manner.

Here are a few additional notes on the content and organization of the book. Firstly, as mentioned above, the amount of information on specific innings has increased significantly overtime. For example, in John Clarkson's time, the first pitcher in this collection who played for the Boston Beaneaters in the late 1800s, pretty much all we have are the names of the batters he faced. In the modern era especially since the mid 2000s, there are a plethora of online data sources, including Pitchf/x, which provides pitch-by-pitch data for all batters faced in a game. This, along with extensive print and online media coverage such as digital streaming of the innings to watch, provides unprecedented information on the minutia of the game. The detail on immaculate innings, therefore, is not the same from beginning to end. One example of this is the addition of tables reviewing each of the nine pitches based on data derived from Pitchf/x; these only appear in the book for entries after 2007 and even then, not all pitchers have these data available. Additionally, I have also provided player statistics for each pitcher, including win-loss records, and earned run average (ERA—career and in some instances, for specific periods). I do so because these are still among the most widely reported statistics, or stats, even though there is increasing recognition of the fact that such stats are much better indicators of team performance, not individual pitching performance per se. For example, while we credit a win to a pitcher, it takes a whole team effort to pull off a victory. One has only to think of Nolan Ryan, who pitched for some pretty terrible teams in his career; his talents as a pitcher are undeniable, yet that alone was not enough to win on some nights. I have also organized the innings into sections, based on chronology and the number of times a perfect inning occurred. These periods do not represent dates of significance to the broader game but are merely for convenience and organization. The last point regarding organization I will make is with regard to the four pitchers who pitched more than one immaculate inning: I elected to violate the chronology and describe each inning attributed to the pitcher at the time of the first recorded perfect inning.

Before beginning, it may be of interest to know how the idea for this book came about, and why a university professor with no background in the game as either a player or a journalist should come to write it. I came to baseball as a fan, not a player (my son has more talent at ten than I ever had). In Canada, the country where I live, baseball is not one of the big sports—we are a nation of hockey players, not ball players. Yet that began to change in 1969 when the Montreal Expos became a National League team. By 1977, when the Toronto Blue Jays joined the American League East, baseball, at last, seemed to have a firm foothold in the Canadian sport landscape. Although only one of those clubs survived the turbulent period following the baseball strike in 1994-95, every spring, we feel the sense of renewal and optimism that Americans feel as the baseball season resumes. For me though, it was not until my thirties (well after both clubs were established) that my love of the sport grew to include a love of its history. I started reading as much as I could on the early history of the game, and I grew to appreciate the nuances of the sport, including the achievements of players and the setting of unusual records related to pitching and hitting. The idea for this book though can be traced directly to the 2013 season and the story of Steve Delabar (one of the pitchers in this book). I was driving home from work and listening to a Toronto AM Sports radio station, the FAN 590, when during a recap of the previous night's contest between the Jays and the Oakland A's, it was noted that Delabar retired the side in the eighth on just nine pitches. The host used the words immaculate inning and I was instantly hooked. I went home and started combing Baseball Reference, Google, any source I could find, trying to learn more. How often does is happen? How many pitchers have done it? I started to wonder if there was a book in all of this. In my day job, I write all the time for scientific journals but I had never written a book on baseball. I soon realized that was about to change, and a history of perfect innings would be my first venture into sports writing. But what does a professor of child health have to say about immaculate innings? In other words, why me and not an ex-player or baseball journalist? One of the great things about baseball writing today is that it is no longer a closed shop or exclusive club. Bill James deserves a lot of the credit for this change. Today, anyone who spends the time can research almost any aspect of this great game and write about it; more and more people from outside the sport are doing just that. The more I researched, the more I realized not only that I had enough material for a book, but that no one else had bothered to write a chronicle of this amazing achievement. Frankly, this continues to surprise me. Given all this, it seemed only right to finish the job. In the pages that follow, I present to you a history of immaculate innings, at least to the end of the 2014 season.

PART I: 1889-1928

John Clarkson
June 4th, 1889

Today, if you want to know the details of a perfect inning, you can go to YouTube and watch the highlights on video or get a pitch-by-pitch break-down on Pitchf/x. While we do not have such records for the early accounts of immaculate innings, we do know this—the first recorded immaculate inning occurred on June 4th, 1889 and the first pitcher was John Clarkson. Clarkson was a pitcher for the Boston Beaneaters. The team may be long forgotten by fans of the game today, but Clarkson, at least among baseball historians, is certainly remembered. The Beaneaters were a National League team, so the first recorded instance of an immaculate inning is credited to this league. But who was John Clarkson and what happened that day?

Born on July 1st, 1861, Clarkson came from a middle class family—his father the owner of a jewelry business. He attended Business school in Boston and subsequently worked for a time in the family shop. His prowess in baseball, already evident in high school where he played as a catcher, meant it would not be long before Clarkson sought a different path than his father. Interestingly, there must have been a collective pas-sion for the game in his family, as he had two brothers who both played baseball for Harvard University.[12] He entered professional baseball, first

---

12 Brian McKenna, "John Clarkson," SABR: http://sabr.org/bioproj/person/47feb015. Retrieved on June 21st, 2013.

with the Worcester Ruby Legs in 1882, then played several seasons with the Chicago White Stockings (1884-1887), Boston Beaneaters (1888-1892) and Cleveland Spiders (1892-1894). He is widely regarded as one of the premiere pitchers of the 19th century, posting several notable achievements. In twelve seasons, his record of 328 wins and 178 loses is truly impressive. In six of these seasons, Clarkson had 30 or more wins, including two seasons where he won more than 40 games: this achievement puts him in two of the top four all-time spots for most wins in a season (53 in 1885 and 49 in 1889). He won the National League pitching Triple Crown (leading the league in wins, strikes and ERA) in 1889. In 1885 and 1889 he pitched over 600 innings, and in back to back seasons (1885 and 1886), he recorded over 300 strikeouts each year. All in all, Clarkson had an impressive career. At least one source ranks Clarkson as the number four pitcher of all time, behind Cy Young, Christy Mathewson, and Lefty Grove.[13] More conservatively, we can at least say he is in the top 100, if not top 50 list of all time pitching greats.[14] He retired from baseball at the age of 33 and was posthumoously inducted into the Hall of Fame in 1963.

With regard to his pitching style, Clarkson's strongest weapon seems to have been his curve ball. His ability to read batters, find weaknesses and adjust accordingly is also noted. He may have also been quite savvy with equipment, exploiting all possible advantages against his opponents. Shiny belt buckles were a particular favorite of his, and on sunny days, when the sun was behind the batter, he took full advantage of the glare.[15]

Clarkson's immaculate inning came in a game against the Philadelphia Quakers in June of 1889. As already noted, 1889 was a good year for the Beantown pitcher. He led the National League that year in wins, ERA, innings pitched, strikeouts, and complete games. But on June 4th in the 3rd inning, Carlson added pitching an immaculate inning to those other accomplishments. The three batters he faced were Jim Fogarty, Sam Thompson, and Sid Farrar. By one account, he would get them all again in the 6[th] inning.[16] Beyond this information, unfortunately, we have little else on record.

---

13 Eric Mikilich, "The Players-John Clarkson" 19[th] Century Baseball: www.19c[b]aseball. com Retrieved August 10[th], 2013

14 Bill James, *The New Bill James Historical Abstract*, Free Press, United States, 2001.

15 Source: http://everything2.com/title/John+Clarkson. Retrieved on Aug 10[th] 2013.

16 *Boston Globe*, June 5[th] 1889.

While 1889 was a personal best for Clarkson, in a career of many achievements on the field, it was a turbulent time in professional baseball. As Warren Goldstein has commented, the history of baseball is more than a record of achievements on the field, it can also be viewed through a political economy lens, where the struggle between labour (ball players) and capital (owners) becomes the dominant theme.[17] By the end of the '89 season, that struggle would reach a boiling point. Since the replacement of the National Association with the National League a decade before, curtailing the rights of players had been the policy of ownership, first under William Hulbert, continuing under the leadership of his young protégé, Albert Spalding.[18] Among the more nefarious policies enacted was the reserve clause, which prevented the inflation of players' salaries by binding them to a single team. Prior to this, player contracts were basically for a single season, renewed at the discretion of the owner each year. There was nothing to stop a player from jumping his contract to go to a rival club willing to pay more for his services—a true open market system for players. The reserve clause prevented this practice, giving owners control and making players little more than chattel to be bought and sold. But by the 1880s, players were beginning to fight back. It was during this time that the first professional union—the Brotherhood of Base Ball Players—was formed. Led by Monte (John) Ward, the union would eventually lead to the Players League Rebellion in 1890: In the year following Clarkson's perfect inning, he and his colleagues would make a bold move and start their own rival league.[19] The league itself was short-lived and in the end, the owners and the reserve clause outlived the player revolt.

After leaving baseball, Clarkson had a second career as a cigar shop owner. Unfortunately, he struggled with mental health problems, suffering at least one nervous breakdown in 1906, which resulted in three years as a patient in various mental institutions. He died in 1909 at the age of 47. The official cause of death was listed as pneumonia.

---

17 Warren Goldstein, *Playing for Keeps: A History of Early Baseball.* Cornell University Press, 1989, pp 1-10.

18 John Thorn, *Baseball in the Garden of Eden: The Secret History of the Early Game.* Simon & Shuster, 2011, pp 154-57.

19 Thorn, Opt Cit.

Rube Waddell
July 1st, 1902

It would be thirteen years before the occurrence of the next immaculate inning. On July 1st, 1902, George Edward "Rube" Waddell, in his first home game for the Philadelphia Athletics, accomplished the feat becoming both the first American League pitcher and the first southpaw (lefty) to pitch a perfect inning.

It seems fitting that this most rare of events was accomplished by a truly unique figure in the history of baseball. By all accounts, Rube Waddell was one of a kind. As with many such interesting historical figures, it is difficult to separate fact from fiction. For example, it was claimed that Rube so loved fires, he would drop everything, including a game he was pitching in, to chase fire engines to the scene of the blaze. There is little evidence to support that this ever happened though. His biography is equally shrouded in controversy. For example, he missed pitching in the 1905 World Series. It is unclear if this is due to an injury (one that ensued over an incident involving a team mate and a straw hat) or whether he had been paid off by gamblers not to show up. According to at many historians, neither account can be fully supported.

There are less contentious, but otherwise quite compelling story lines concerning his professional career. Adding to the mythology of Rube, for example, is the interesting timing of both his birth and death—born on a Friday the 13th in 1876, his life came to a tragic, if not heroic end, on April

Fool's Day in 1914 at the very young age of 37. His personal demons are also well known. His drinking is certainly well documented. It also seems possible, as Bill James has suggested, that Rube may have been autistic or suffering from attention deficit disorder. With the disorder unknown at the time, diagnosis would have been impossible. There are certainly stories of his "distractibility": fans were able to hold his attention by flashing shiny objects. His impulsivity and aggressiveness were displayed through numerous stories of fights with teammates. A neurodevelopmental disorder (attention deficit disorder; autism spectrum disorder) would certainly explain some of these behaviours. He also had the reputation of being child-like: Rube once missed a game he was scheduled to pitch in to play a game of marbles with a group of children. I could not find any reference to the outcome of the game, or his prowess as a marble player, but I suspect he was formidable (and hopefully, not ill-tempered with his young fans).[20]

Despite all this, Rube had a remarkable career as a ball player and there are numerous accolades and records to prove it. He was talented enough for Athletics manager and baseball great Connie Mack not only to put up with his strange antics (at least for a while), but also to say he had more "stuff" than anyone he had ever seen.[21] He would many times lead either the American or National League in strikeouts, ERA and wins throughout his career. Notably, he led the American League in strikeouts from 1902 to 1907. In 1905, he won the Triple Crown for pitching (leading the league in wins, strikes and ERA). He holds three all time records: ranked 11th on the MLB all-time ERA list (2.16), 20th on all time WHIP list (1.102) and 19th for all time shutouts (50 career).[22] His career win-loss record was 193-143, with 2,316 strikeouts to his credit in 407 games played. A result of all this and more, Rube was elected to the Baseball Hall of Fame in 1946. About his pitching, it was said he possessed both a great fastball and curve, and that his accuracy was laser-like. Together, this was enough to ensure his place in the record books, and in this collection.

---

20 Steven A. King, "Strange Career of Rube Waddell," SABR: http://sabr.org/research/strangest-month-strange-career-rube-waddell#footnote2_38jw3mb. Retrieved on August 9th 2013.

21 "Rube Waddell Hall of Fame Page," Baseball Hall of Fame: http://baseballhall.org/hof/waddell-rube. Retrieved on December 23rd, 2014.

22 "Rube Waddell Player Page," Baseball Reference: http://www.baseball-reference.com/players/w/wadderu01.shtml. Retrieved on December 23rd, 2014.

On the matter of the inning itself, it was the 2nd of July in 1902 that Rube faced the Baltimore Orioles. Connie Mack's recent acquisition did not disappoint on that day. Although we have limited information about the specifics of the game, here is what we do know for sure. In the 3rd inning, he faced: Billy Gilbert, Harry Howell and Jack Cronin. In order, they went down, striking out the side on just nine pitches. In addition to an immaculate 3rd, Rube struck out a total of 13 Orioles that day, allowing only 2 hits. The following tribute to Rube and his performance in that game was published in the *Philadelphia Inquiry* a short time later:

> *Up to the bat the Orioles rose, his face was filled with glee*
> *There're various brands of glee you've never seen before.*
> *"Strike one," the umpire cried, "strike two"—*
> *the umpire said "strike three."*
> *But you've seldom seen those kinds of strikes before.*
> *For when Reuben twirls the sphere*
> *The Planets shrink in fear.*
> *And the sinuous sea serpent*
> *Its sorrow tries to drown.*
> *Then the cyclone hides its head,*
> *And the birds go right to bed*
> *For there's doings on the Diamond*
> *when Reuben comes to town.[23]*

An immaculate inning in any era is an impressive accomplishment, but we should not forget what the game was like in Rube's time. Today, foul balls can be called strikes when the batter has two strikes against him. In 1902 though, no such rule existed. In other words, there was no contact with any of Rube's nine pitches—perhaps the epitome of a perfect inning?

On April 1st, 1914, just a few months before the start of World War I, Rube died from tuberculosis while in a sanatorium. It is believed his tuberculosis was the result of successive bouts of pneumonia, the first of which resulted from prolonged exposure to icy water when Rube piled sandbags fighting to save the town of Hickman, Kentucky from a severe spring flood

---

23 "The Immaculate Inning: Rube Waddel," The Immaculate Inning Blog: http://www. immaculateinning.com/2008/08/immaculate-inning-rube-waddell.html.   Retrieved on August 9, 2013.

in 1912. The day after his death, the following poem by R.B. Pixley was published in *the Milwaukee Sentinel*:

> *They tell me Rube Waddell is dead—*
> *Well—he was a game old scout—*
> *The kind that fights till the last ball's pitched*
> *And the umpire says: "You're out!"*
>
> *The man on the first wire says the news*
> *Just came in from San Antone—*
> *Well — the game has lost a big league star,*
> *And as good as league could own.*
>
> *You see, I followed the Rube for years*
> *And gloried in his skill*
> *The way a fellow who just falls short*
> *Of athletic prowess will;*
>
> *I watched the box scores day by day*
> *And looked for the bottom line—*
> *The names of the sluggers topped each list,*
> *But I picked the Rube's for mine,*
>
> *And I counted the number of times at bat*
> *And the number of strikeouts there*
> *I wasn't afraid to reckon up,*
> *For I knew that the Rube was there.*
>
> *I followed the Rube in his palmy days,*
> *When he mowed them down like wheat,*
> *And I clung to those memories when the ways*
> *Of the swift pace had him beat;*
>
> *And when the big leagues turned him loose,*
> *And now that he's answered the final call,*
> *I never could think, and I can't think now*
> *Of Rube Waddell in minor ball.*

So do me a favor, you men who write
Of the stars who rule this age;
When you write the story of Rube Waddell
Let charity turn the page

Which tells of the times when the Rube went bad
And lost to John Barleycorn.
For if ever man's life was a written book
Many pages of each would be torn;

Just recall the days when he stood out there
And battled a howling mob—
Just tell of the days when the Rube was right
And you'll say he was on the job;

The Rube was a man in his build and strength,
But at heart he was only a child,
And the best of the children of men are weak
And the best may grow reckless and wild.

Well — the man on the first wire says the news
Just came that the Rube was out;
Let it go as it lays, for the game is fair...
But...the Rube was a game old Scout![24]

---

24 R.B. Pixley reprinted in Baseball Almanac: http://www.baseball-almanac.com/players/ player.php?p=wadderu01. Retrieved August on 10, 2013.

Pat Ragan
October 5th, 1914

The third recorded immaculate inning occurred twelve years after Rube Waddell's on October 5th, 1914. The times had indeed changed, especially in the world outside the United States and professional baseball. World War I was well into its first year, and although it would be several more before America declared war on Germany and its allies (April of 1917), stories of the war were unquestionably big news across the country. Major League Baseball had yet to feel the effects of losing so many young men to wartime efforts.

Unlike the first two pitchers in this collection, we know much less about the hurler at the centre of this event. Don Carlos Patrick Ragan was born on the 15th of November in 1885 in Blanchard, Iowa. He died at the age of 70, while living in Los Angeles. We know that he was a starting pitcher, a righty, made his Major League debut with the Cincinnati Reds on April 21st, 1909, and that he played his last game, as a Philadelphia Philly, on July 5th, 1923 at the age of 37. In between, he played for five other teams: the Chicago Cubs (1909), the Brooklyn Robins (1911-15), the Boston Braves (1915-19), the New York Giants (1919) and the Chicago White Sox (1919). His record provides some insight into why we know so little else. Overall, he had a career record of 77-104. He posted 680 strikeouts, pitched 93 complete games, 12 shutouts and had an ERA of 2.99.[25] A

---

25 "Pat Ragan Player Page," Baseball Reference: http://www.baseball-reference.com/players/r/raganpa01.shtml. Retrieved on December 22, 2014.

33

career that, unlike the first two pitchers in this collection, pretty much ensured he would not be admitted to the Hall in Cooperstown. Ring Lardner, the sports columnist and novelist, gave his opinion of Ragan through the fictitious letters of his popular character, bush league baseball player "Jack Keefe." I paraphrase here: the White Sox demonstrated just how desperate they have become by signing Pat Ragan, a player who had made his way through every other club in the National League.[26] High praise this was not. Ragan's only claim to fame is that he was the third pitcher in professional baseball to pitch an immaculate inning; and the second pitcher from the National League to do so.

Interestingly, the inning itself does stand out as unique in the annals of immaculate innings. Not for Ragan's pitching but for his less than sportsmanlike conduct during the feat. The contest was between the Brooklyn Robins, Ragan's team, and the first place Boston Braves. The day before, the Braves had trounced the home team handily, taking the contest 15-2 (in a game that lasted just over one hour). In game two, the Robins had managed to keep it closer, but still trailed the Braves 4-1 when Ragan took the hill in the 8th inning. It appeared that Ragan sensed he had something special that day, and decided to make a true show for the fans in attendance right from the start. After the first pitch, a strike to Possum Whitted, he "tossed" his hat (I take this to mean he tipped or removed his hat in a gesture of thanks) to the fans seated behind the Braves dugout, reacting to an imagined applauding crowd. After pitching a second strike, he repeated the act, this time to the other side of the stand. By the third time, the applause was real.[27]

The act continued for each of the three pitches to the second batter of the inning, Butch Schimdt. Apparently, now to the bemusement of fans and players alike, the latter group described as convulsing with laughter, both Whitted and Schmidt went down without swinging. Ragan's antics seemed to stop once Red Smith took his position in the batter's box, as perhaps he finally sensed he was on the verge of achieving something very special. Unlike his teammates, Red swung on every pitch, missing all three.

We may indeed judge Ragan's performance harshly due to his antics and shameless showmanship, but in 1909, basebal, this behaviour was not at all out of the ordinary. Regardless, Ragan's team ended up losing the

---

26 George W. Hitlon ed., *The Annotated Baseball Stories of GW Lardner. 1914-1919*, Stanford University Press, Stanford Cal. 1995, pp 305-306.

27 "Pat Ragan – Immanculate Inning," Immaculate Inning Blog: http://www.immaculateinning. com/2008/08/immaculate-inning-pat-ragan.html. Retrieved on Aug 15, 2013.

game: the final contest in an otherwise mediocre season. On a personal level, Ragan accomplished something remarkable. Though most of his career was largely unremarkable, Ragan's stylish immaculate inning distinguishes him from the brotherhood of pitchers who achieved the same.

Before continuing, it is important to note one more connection that links Ragan to a significant historical event in baseball. He was listed on the pitching roster of the 1919 Chicago White Sox, the same year of the infamous Black Sox Scandal where eight players (among them, well-known players like Shoeless Joe Jackson) were accused of throwing World Series games for money. Ragan, though, was not one of the eight, and in fact, only played one game for the Sox that year. In *Twelfth Night*, Shakespeare wrote: "Some are born great, some achieve greatness, and some have greatness thrust upon them." In the case of Ragan, we may add: others make history by virtue of proximity.

Joe Oeschger
September 8th, 1921

Changes in the character and make-up of baseball over the decades frequently offer a reflection of broader cultural changes occurring across America. In the 1920s, America was growing rapidly, primarily due to an influx of immigration from Western and Eastern Europe. The fourth pitcher of a perfect inning, Joe Oeschger, is a primary example of the emerging diversity of the country. A child of immigrant parents, Oeschger (pronounced "Eshker") pitched his immaculate inning in 1921 during a period of great optimism, particularly for first generation Americans. Baseball, in particular, experienced the broad effects of the post-war boom and influx of diversity, as its popularity skyrocketed amongst immigrant communities looking to engage with America's pastime. Interest in the game was aided dramatically thanks to dedicated sports pages in newspapers and the growing popularity of radio. Transformation in sports media changed how the game was consumed, and elevated the fame of the era's stars, like Babe Ruth, to new heights. Sports historians would later dub it the 'Golden Era' of the game. Not only a golden era for baseball, the decade was eventually called the 'Roaring '20s', as a hopeful and freewheeling attitude pervaded much of the art and film of the time. While this optimism would dramatically evaporate by the end of the decade, it provided the backdrop for the fourth recorded immaculate inning.

The son of Swiss immigrants, Oeschger, one of six children, was born in Chicago on May 24th, 1892. When he was 8 years old, the Oeschger family moved from the big city to the country, Ferndale, California to be exact, where Joe's father bought some land and eventually established a dairy ranch. Joe's baseball recorded career seems to have begun during his time at Ferndale High School, but he also played for Saint Mary's College in California, graduating from that school in 1914. One of his schoolmates, Eddie Burns, had already signed with the Philadelphia Phillies in 1913, and when Joe graduated a year later, Burns encouraged the young pitcher to sign with his team.[28]

Oeschger's career in the Majors spanned twelve seasons, from 1914 to 1925. He made his Major League debut with the Philadelphia Phillies on April 21st, 1914, losing to the Boston Braves 4-3 (a team he would later join and pitch his best seasons with). 'California Joe', a name he received from Philly sportswriters, left the team in 1919 at the age of 27. He was traded twice that season, first to the New York Giants, and then to the Braves. While with the Braves, Oeschger won his first game with a shutout against the Chicago Cubs (1-0). He pitched his last game for the Brooklyn Robins, on September 6th, 1925. Overall, he had an 82 -116 record, with a 3.81 ERA and 535 strikeouts.

Oeschger was best known for his endurance, pitching the longest game ever in professional baseball. The game in question occurred between the Braves and the Brooklyn Robins on May 1st, 1920, shortly after Oeschger had been traded to Braves. The game was an epic pitching duel between Oeschger and Leon Cadore of the Robins, with both pitching into the 26th inning. At this point, the umpires called the game because of darkness. Remarkably, both pitchers held the score to 1-1. Even more remarkable, Oeschger pitched a perfect game over the last 9 innings. He gave up only 9 hits in the whole game, ahead of Cadore, who surrendered just 15 hits.

While pitching an immaculate inning may seem a lesser feat than this epic spectacle of endurance, it is still notable to be ranked among the small number of pitchers to retire the side on nine pitches. The event in question occurred on September 8th, 1921. Osechger was pitching for the Boston Braves in a game against the Philadelphia Athletics. While there is no box-

---

28 John Green, "Joe Oeschger," SABR: http://sabr.org/bioproj/person/69[b]c1732. Retrieved on December 22, 2014.

score for the contest, it is known that in the 4th inning Bevo LeBourveau, Cy Williams and Ed Konetchy all struck out in order on nine pitches.

After baseball, Joe had a long career as an educator, spending twenty-eight years at Portola Junior High School. He taught physical education and health, and eventually retired as vice-principal. He died at the age of 94 in Rohnert, California.

Sloppy Thurston
August 22nd, 1923

It would be just over a year before the next immaculate inning was pitched. With a name like Hollis John "Sloppy" Thurston, one would expect a colorful story or two about the fifth pitcher in baseball history to join the rarefied few to achieve this feat. Unfortunately, no such stories could be found.

The facts we can be certain of are that Sloppy Thurston was born on June 2, 1899, in Fremont, Nebraska (pop. 7,200 inhabitants when Thurston was born). His professional career began with the St. Louis Browns in 1923. He was then traded the same year to the Chicago White Sox, where he played for four years (1923-26). After one year with the Washington Senators in '27, Thurston finished his nine-year professional career with the Brooklyn Robins/Dodgers (1930-33). He finished his career with an 89-86 win-loss record, a 4.24 ERA, and 306 strikeouts.[29]

Thurston was known as a screwball pitcher.[30] The screwball or "screwgie," as it was sometimes called, is a pitch that breaks in the opposite direction of a curveball or slider. When thrown by a right-hander like Thurston, the screwball broke from left to right (from the perspective of the pitch-

29 "Sloppy Thurston". Baseball-Reference.com. Retrieved on October 29, 2013.

30 Bill James and Rob Neyer, *The Neyer/James Guide to Pitchers: An Historical Compendium of Pitching, Pitchers, and Pitches*. Simon and Schuster. p. 52.

er's mound), resulting in a pitch that came down and in to a righty, and down and away to a lefty. This description reveals why the term fade-away is often used to describe the screwball. Rob Neyer and Peter Morris have argued that the version of the screwball popular during Thurston's time (the 1920s) was actually more of a sinker, and differed from the screwball popularized by Carl Hubbell.[31] Babe Ruth believed that the innovation of the screwball was a direct response to the banning of the spitball.[32]

Regardless of whether Thurston's pitch is better described as a screwball or sinker, it played a significant part in him becoming the second pitcher in the American League to strike three consecutive batters out on nine pitches. The inning occurred on August 22, 1923, against the Philadelphia Athletics, when Thurston faced Beauty McGowan, Chick Galloway, and Sammy Hale (Beauty rivals Sloppy for best nickname in this entry). Again, in the absence of a boxscore, there is little else to report. What is noteworthy, however, is that Sloppy's perfect 12th was the first of only two recorded in extra innings.

Neither the Chicago White Sox nor the Athletics went beyond the regular season in '22. The World Series that year was between the New York Giants and the New York Yankees, which the Giants took in five games. As is often the case, 's immaculate inning proved inconsequential, at least in relation to the success of his club in the bigger picture of an entire season.

Sloppy Thurston lived to be 74, passing away on September 14th, 1973, in Los Angeles, California. He had lived to see his old club sign slugger Dick Allen to a three-year contract for $750,000, making him the highest paid player in Major League history at that time. One wonders what must have gone through his mind, having played during a time when the reserve clause prevented players from negotiating better salaries, and having worked for the notoriously "frugal" owner, Charles Comiskey. Like many of his contemporaries, he would not live long enough to see Marvin Miller successfully overturn the reserve clause in 1975.

---

31 Ibid, p.115 and David Schoenfield, "Baseball's greatest pitches of all-time", ESPN. com (May 15, 2007):

32 Babe Ruth, *Babe's Ruth's Own Book of Baseball*, p78. Cited in Peter Morris, *A Game of Inches*, p. 116.

Dazzy Vance
September 24th, 1924

More immaculate innings occurred in the 1920s than in the period since the first recorded instance back in 1889. The sixth pitcher to record a perfect inning, and the third of the decade, was Hall of Famer Charles Arthur "Dazzy" Vance. Born in Orient, Iowa on March 4, 1891, Vance earned the nickname "Dazzy" thanks to his dazzling fastball. This pitch would propel him to an stand-out Major League career filled with outstanding achievements.

A right-handed pitcher and batter, Vance first appeared in the big leagues with the Pittsburgh Pirates on April 16th, 1915. He played for five clubs over a sixteen-year career, which spanned from 1915 to 1935: the Pirates (1915), Yankees (1915 and again in 1918), Brooklyn Robins/Dodgers (1922-32, 1935), St Louis Cardinals (1933), and Cincinnati Reds (1934). He was the only National League pitcher to lead the league in strikeouts seven seasons in a row (1922-28). He also won the pitcher's Triple Crown (28 wins, 262 strikeouts and an ERA of 2.16) in 1924, the same year he was also named the National League MVP. Three times he led the league in ERA (1924, 1928, 1930), had the most wins in a single season twice (1924, 1925), and pitched a no-hitter on September 13th, 1925. He retired from the game with a win-loss record of 197-140, a career ERA of 3.24, and 2,045 strikeouts. Overall, his career statistics make it easy to see why the Baseball Writers of America voted him into the Hall of Fame in 1955.

However, Vance was not always at the top of his game. Prior to his Hall of Fame Major League career, he had a less than impressive ten-year minor league career, which began in 1912 when he was 21. A friendly poker game between minor league teammates one night in New Orleans has been identified as the crucial turning point that changed the fortunes of the struggling 29-year-old.[33] It was during this game that Dazzy Vance banged his arm on the edge of the table while collecting his winnings. Feeling immediate, intense pain, Vance thought little of it until the next morning when his arm continued to feel sore. Seeking medical attention, the attending doctor diagnosed a pre-existing elbow injury as the underlying cause of his pain (banging his arm was merely a trigger or exacerbating factor). What the treatment actually was (or the diagnosis for that matter) is not part of the historical record, although Bill James has speculated that the likely intervention was the removal of bone chips and scar tissue from the elbow.[34] Post surgery, Vance went on to win 21 games for the Pelicans in 1921. The next year, he was back in the Majors, this time for good.

While the second half of his career was marked by numerous achievements, Vance was also involved in one of the most infamous gaffes in baseball history—the "three men on third" blunder.[35] On August 15th, 1926, the "Daffiness Boys", which included Vance, Chick Fewster, and Babe Herman, all managed to end up on the same base at the same time during a single play. [36] Chick was on first, Vance on second, when Babe Herman hit a long ball to right field. By the time Babe had rounded second on his way to third, Fewster, having not yet reached third and Vance, having just passed it, looked up to see the third base coach yelling "go back." Both Vance and Fewster heeded the call but Herman, the player to whom the coach was actually yelling to, kept coming. So, with all three men now on third, an easy double play was made by the opposing team's third baseman. Vance remained in, declared safe for having arrived ahead of the others. John Lardner nicely summarized the incident: "Babe Herman did

---

33 Charles F. Faber, "Dazzy Vance," SABR: http://sabr.org/bioproj/person/5c1f²c75. Retrieved on November 2, 2013.

34 Fred Lieb, "Dazzy Vance, Hall of Fame Pitching Star, Dies at 69," *The Sporting News* (February 22, 1961) reprinted in www.TheDeadBallEra.com

35 Edward J. Rielly. *Baseball: An Encyclopedia of Popular Culture.* University of Nebraska Press, pp. 36.

36 Faber, Op Cit.

not triple into a triple play, but he doubled into a double play, which is the next best thing."[37] To his credit, Vance was the only player of the three in the right place at the right time.

Like many pitchers of those early days of modern baseball, Vance relied on both raw talent, and a certain degree of showmanship and props to gain an advantage over his opponents. Indeed, while Dazzy may have been short for dazzling, we might also describe his pitching style has bedazzled. Vance's jersey was described as "tattered" and "sweat-stained", and opposing players accused him of slitting his right sleeve, creating a visual distraction caused by the waving strips of flannel that accompanied his follow-through on a fastball pitch.[38] Vance denied that was his intention, claiming instead it was just a lucky jersey. According to Casey Stengel, who faced Vance many times as a batter, it was not a tattered sleeve that fooled hitters it was his stuff.

Dazzy Vance was the sixth pitcher in baseball, and the fourth National League player, to record an immaculate inning. On September 24th, 1924, during the 2nd inning, he retired Sam Bohne, Bubbles Hargrave, and Eppa Rixey in order on nine pitches. Vance's Dodgers went on to beat the Chicago Cubs 6-5. For the entire season, he recorded 262 strikeouts, leading the National League and more than doubling the second and third-ranked pitchers (Burleigh Grimes with 135 and Dolf Luque with 86).

Vance died on February 16th, 1961, from a heart attack, just two weeks short of his 70th birthday. He appeared to have been in good health and enjoying life right to the end. Just a month before his death, he had played baseball in St. Petersburg Florida in an old-timers game.[39]

---

37 "Babe Herman," Baseball Reference: http://www.baseball-reference.com/bullpen/ Babe_Herman. Retrieved on November 8, 2013.

38 Faber, Op. cit.

39 Faber, Op. cit.

Lefty Grove
August 23rd, 1928 & September 27th, 1928

Is Lefty Grove the greatest pitcher of all time? Whether you agree or not, you would be hard-pressed to find anyone to argue that he should not at least be in the conversation. The fact that he still holds the top spot in records such as win percentage among 300-game winners, and ERA titles, speaks to his dominance. I might add, humbly, so does his immaculate inning record. Not only did he achieve this feat of perfection, he did so twice in just over a month. As a result, he became the first pitcher to record two perfect innings, and the only pitcher to record back-to-back immaculate innings in the same season.

Robert Moses Grove was born in Lonaconing, Maryland on March 6th, 1900. Grove would have been expected to follow both his father and brothers to the mines but unlike them, he did not last long in that occupation. He is famously quoted as saying to his father, "Dad, I didn't put that coal in here, and I hope I don't have to take no more of her out."[40] It does not appear to be baseball, however, that distracted a young Grove. By at least one account, Grove would be 19 years old before he played anything close to the game we would recognize today.[41] It was Jack Dunn, owner of the minor

---

40 Jim Kaplan, "Lefty Grove," SABR: http://sabr.org/bioproj/person/8bc0a9e1. Retrieved on November 1, 2014.

41 Kaplan, Ibid.

league Baltimore Orioles, who first spotted Grove and eventually signed him to a contract. Dunn certainly had a good eye for talent, as he also discovered Babe Ruth. Grove would join the team in 1920 and play for four seasons in the International League. His performance would catch the eye of many big league clubs, but in the absence of a minor league draft and contracts which bound players firmly to owners, Dunn was able to hold onto Grove for a number of seasons, refusing multiple offers until finally he agreed to sell his young star to an old friend, Connie Mack, the owner/manager of the Philadelphia Athletics, for $100,600 (reportedly $600 more than the Cubs and Dodgers had offered).[42] Grove debuted for the Athletics on April 14th, 1925. Many have pondered what the addition of four years in the Majors could have done to the already impressive career stats Grove achieved.

From the late '20s to the '30s, Connie Mack's A's were a dominant force in Major League Baseball and Grove was an essential part of the club's success. The Athletics won the pennant three consecutive seasons from 1929 to 1931, and won back-to-back World Series in 1929 and 1930. Grove's numbers in that period place him comfortably at the top of all other pitchers in the era. From 1929 to 1931, his win-loss record was 20-6, 28-5, and 31-4, respectively, placing him at the top for win-loss percentage in the American League (.769, .848 and .886). From 1929 to 1932, he had the lowest ERA (2.81, 2.54, 2.06 and 2.84) in the American League and was first overall in strikeouts (170, 209, 175 and 188). In 1931, he was awarded league MVP, an honour rarely bestowed on a pitcher.[43]

In terms of his make-up as a pitcher, Grove had a slightly unfair reputation for being a one-pitch hurler, with a devastating fastball. Charlie Gehringer gave a vivid picture of the speed of Grove's fastball, declaring it "was so fast that by the time you'd made up your mind whether it would be a strike or not, it just wasn't there anymore."[44] Arthur 'Bugs' Baer described it with a bit more flair, remarking: "Lefty Grove could throw a lamb chop past a wolf."[45]Although he relied heavily on the fastball, particularly early

---

42 Kaplan, Ibid.

43 "Lefty Grove," Baseball Reference: http://www.baseball-reference.com/players/g/grovele01.shtml?redir. Retrieved on November 1, 2014.

44 Quote is from Charlie Gehringer in "Lefty Grove," Baseball Hall of Fame: http://baseballhall.org/hof/grove-lefty. Retrieved on October 30, 2014.

45 Arthur "Bugs" Baer quoted in Red Smith, "Terrible-Tempered Mr. Grove," Joseph Veccione ed., *New York Times Book of Sports Legends*. Touchstone, 1992, pp. 107.

in his career, Grove was certainly not a one-pitch pitcher. He also possessed a curve ball, which proved particularly effective in the 1931 World Series.[46] Later in his career, he would add a forkball to his collection of pitches.[47] On top of this, his fastball not only had great velocity, but great movement. It was therefore, also Grove's ability to place the ball that fooled batters. The fact he was left-handed also made his stuff all the more challenging for hitters.

Connie Mack was both a brilliant baseball man and an astute business owner. By 1933, his A's had slipped in the standings and so too had attendance. Like so many times throughout his career, Mack would respond to the dip in profits by selling off his top talent to make room for younger, cheaper prospects. This time, it would be Grove, along with Max Bishop and Rube Walberg, who were traded to Boston to make way for much less established, and therefore, much less costly, players. Grove would stay with the Red Sox until his retirement in 1941, continuing his winning record and again leading the league in ERA four out of five years from 1935 to 1939.

We do not have a lot of detail on Grove's successive immaculate innings, but there are key pieces of information available. The first came on August 23rd, 1928, in a game against the Cleveland Indians in the 2nd inning. Grove faced and retired in order: Ed Morgan, Luther Harvel and Martin Autry. Grove also got the win that day, as the A's beat the Indians 3-1. Just over a month later on September 27th, this time in a game against the Chicago White Sox, he would repeat the feat, this time retiring Moe Berg, Tommy Thomas and Johnny Mostil on nine strikes in the 7th inning. Again, Grove would get the win, beating the White Sox 5-3 that day. As I noted above, Grove was the first pitcher to record two perfect innings and the only one to achieve both in the same season. Much later, fellow Hall of Famers, Sandy Koufax, Nolan Ryan and Randy Johnson would also record 2 perfect innings, but none would do so in the same season.

Grove made his final appearance for the Red Sox on September 28th, 1941. His career win-loss record was 300-141, a win-loss percentage of .680,./ which is ranked 8th on the all-time list (although none of the seven pitchers ahead him pitched more than 236 games). He had a career ERA

---

46 Kaplan, Op Cit.

47 Bill James and Rob Neyer, The Neyer/James Guide to Pitchers: An Historical Compendium of Pitching, Pitchers and Pitches. Touchstone, 2004, pp.225.

of 3.06 and 2,266 strikeouts to his credit. He made six All-Star Game appearances (1933; 1935-1939), pitched on two World Series Teams, was an MVP in 1931, and a two-time Triple Crown Winner (1930, 1931). He was inducted into the Baseball Hall of Fame in 1947, capturing more than two-thirds of the vote on the third ballot (76.4% to be precise). In terms of character, Grove has been described as truculent and there are many recorded instances of angry outbursts directed at team members he felt were not trying hard enough and pay-back pitches to hitters he felt had got the better of him (which by his record, were few). [48] He lived to be 75 years of age.

48 Kaplan, Op Cit.

PART II: 1953-1969

Billy Hoeft
September 7th, 1953

After Lefty Grove's back-to-back immaculate innings, the baseball gods decided to right the imbalance of an improbable event striking twice in the same season by blocking it from happening for the next twenty-five years. The gods smiled once again though, this time on Billy Hoeft, late in the season on September 7th, 1953, during a contest between his Detroit Tigers and the Chicago White Sox.

William Frederick Hoeft was born on May 17th, 1932, in Oshkosh, Wisconsin (parents of young children will recognize the name of that town immediately). Another lefty, like his predecessor Grove, however, further comparisons to the Hall of Famer leave Hoeft falling well short. Hoeft made his Major League debut on April 18th, 1952, for the Detroit Tigers. In 1955, his play would earn him a spot on the American League All-Star Team. The following year, he became the first lefty Tiger pitcher since Hal Newhouser to win 20 games in a single season. He also led the American League with 7 shutouts in '55. He played in Detroit for eight seasons before being traded to the Red Sox in 1959. His stay in Boston was very short-lived (playing just three games); he was again traded to the Orioles, where he stayed until 1962. From 1963 to 1966, he played for three different teams—the Milwaukee Brewers, Cubs and Giants—before playing his final game on September 25th, 1966 for San Francisco. By the end of his career, Hoeft finished with a losing record (97-101), a 3.94 ERA, and 1,140 strikeouts. As a relief pitcher, a role he principally held from 1962 to the end of his career, he had 33 saves. Overall, his best seasons as a lefty reliever were with the Orioles, posting an ERA of 2.02 in 1961, and following with four wins and seven saves the following season with the Birds.[49]

Hoeft's perfect inning against the White Sox happened in the top of the 7th inning. He retired in order: Jim Rivera, Mike Fornieles and Chico Carrasquel. Rivera and Fornieles were hitting in the 8th and 9th spot that game, while Carrasquel was batting first. He would pitch all 9 innings and take the win (4-2), recording 7 strikeouts and holding the Sox to just 8 hits. According to the boxscore, Rivera struck-out looking, while both Fornieles and Carrasquel simply "struck out." At that point in the game, the Sox were holding a 1-run lead over the Tigers. In the bottom of that inning, the Tigers scored 3 runs, and held a 2-run lead for the rest of the game to secure their 82nd win of the season.

Hoeft died on a Tuesday at the age of 77 (March 16th 2010), in Canadian Lakes, Michigan. His hometown newspaper, the *Oshkosh Northwestern*, published a tribute from a fellow high school baseball teammate that remembered Hoeft as simply an "outstanding pitcher and also a very good guy."[50] Hoeft's old teammate also credited him for putting Oshkosh baseball on the map.

49 "Billy Hoeft Player Page," Baseball Reference: http://www.baseball-reference.com/ players/h/hoeftbi01.shtml. Retrieved on December 24, 2014.

50 Doug Zellmer, "Hoeft Turned Young Brilliance Into Solid Major-League Career" *The Oshkosh Northwestern* as reprinted in: https://groups.google.com/forum/#!topic/alt. obituaries/GublE0vJCfU. Retrieved on August 3, 2014.

Robin Roberts
April 17th, 1956

Another Hall of Famer to pitch an immaculate inning was Robin Roberts, who at the time of the great feat was a pitcher for the Philadelphia Phillies. He was just one of three pitchers to record a perfect inning in the 1950s.

Born on September 30th, 1926, Robin Evans Roberts was one of six children, born to a farming family in rural Illinois. By at least one account, he was not interested in farm work, but always had a ball in his hand ready to play.[51] During the Second World War, he made his way from Springfield to East Lansing Michigan, first as part of training for the Army Air Corps, and later as a student at Michigan State College. His first seasons at college were spent as a captain of the basketball team, where he earned three varsity letters. Baseball did not come naturally to Roberts, as he failed at early attempts to play first base and in the outfield. But Michigan State coach John Kobs took notice of Robert's strong arm and encouraged him to try pitching. It was not long before he thrived at the position.[52]

Roberts made his debut in the Majors for the Phillies on June 18th, 1948. He would play with that club for fourteen seasons from 1948 to 1961 before moving to Baltimore (via the Yankees who signed and released him before

51 Ralph Berger, "Robin Roberts," SABR: http://sabr.org/bioproj/person/3262b1eb. Retrieved on October 13, 2014.

52 Berger, Ibid.

he played a single game), where he would play four seasons from 1962 to 1965. He finished his career with the Chicago Cubs, playing his final game on September 3rd, 1966. Roberts' career lasted so long (nineteen seasons) that he is the only pitcher in Major League history to beat all three Braves franchises in their home ballparks in Boston, Milwaukee and Atlanta. In the beginning of his career (1948-1951), Roberts was known for three pitches: a rising fastball, slow curve and the occasional sinker. However, after '51, Roberts expanded his arsenal of pitches adding a hard curve. As is often the case with player records from this era, there are discrepancies regarding what kinds of pitches he actually threw. In his personal view, Robins believed he was essentially a fastball pitcher, with a curve and a change-up used as backup options. He also felt his curve was often mischaracterized as a slider, which he said was due to it breaking a little slower than his usual curve ball.[53]

Over his career, he posted a 286-245 record, 3.41 ERA and 2,357 strikeouts over 4,688.2 innings and 676 games. A seven-time All-Star, Roberts was the top pitcher in the National League from '50 to '55 without question. Today, with pitch counts and expanded bullpens, starting pitchers rarely complete games, and are usually pulled after either 100 pitches or reaching the 7th inning. Robins has been described as the last of a breed of pitchers who actually completed games as a starter, with 305 complete games to his credit over his long career.[54]

At the height of his power as a starter, Roberts pitched an immaculate inning against the Dodgers at Ebbets Field on April 17th, 1956. In the bottom of the 6th inning, with the Phillies ahead 7-5, Roberts took the mound to face the bottom of the order: Carl Furillo, Charlie Neal and Sandy Amorós. All three struck out swinging, with just nine pitches thrown. The Phillies eventually beat the Dodgers 8-6. Roberts pitched the whole game, allowing 5 earned runs on 9 hits, striking out 4 and earning his second win of the season.[55]

On March 21st, 1962, the Phillies retired Roberts' number 36 during a pre-game ceremony before a spring-training game against the Yankees

---

53 Source for descriptions on pitches: James and Neyer Ibid, p.360.

54 "Robin Roberts," Baseball Reference: http://www.baseball-reference.com/players/r/roberro01.shtml?redir. Retrieved on October 13, 2014.

55 "Philadelphia Phillies vs Brooklyn Dodgers. April 17th, 1956," Baseball Reference: http://www.baseball-reference.com/boxes/BRO/BRO195604170.shtml. Retrieved on October 13, 2014

in Clearwater Florida. He was inducted into the Hall of Fame in 1976, with more than 85% of the vote on the fourth ballot. On his plaque, he is described as a "tireless worker who never missed a start in decade of the fifties."[56] Bill Giles, Chairmen of the Phillies, had this to say about his old ace: "When I think of Robin there is definitely one word that comes quickly to mind: Class. He was a class act both on and off the field. He was definitely one of the most consistent quality pitchers of all time, and the way he lived his life was exemplary. Every young baseball player should model their life after Robin."[57] It is easy to see why Roberts, given his long career and work ethic, has been described as both a star and a journeyman player.[58] In a career after baseball that included color commentating for Philly broadcasts, coaching at the University of South Florida, touring with an exhibition professional basketball team (the Robin Roberts All-Stars) and even making a TV appearance on *What's My Line*, Roberts passed away on May 6th, 2010 at the age 83. As a final tribute, the Phillies wore a commemorative patch with number 36 on their jerseys for the remainder of the 2010 season.

---

56 "Robin Roberts," Baseball Hall of Fame: http://baseballhall.org/hof/roberts-robin. Retrieved on October 13, 2014.

57 Hall of Fame, Ibid.

58 Berger, Ibid.

Jim Bunning
August 2ⁿᵈ, 1959

James Paul David "Jim" Bunning was born on October 23rd, 1931. A son of Southgate Kentucky, he graduated from St. Xavier High School in Cincinnati (1949), and received a bachelor's degree in economics from Xavier University. A right-handed starting pitcher, Bunning made his debut with the Detroit Tigers on July 20th, 1955 (signed by the club as an amateur free agent in 1950). He would play for four clubs over the course of seventeen seasons: the Detroit Tigers (1955-63); the Phillies (1964-67; 1970-71); the Pittsburgh Pirates (1968-1969), and the Los Angeles Dodgers (1969). He led the American League in wins in 1957, topped the league in strikeouts three times (1959, 1960 and 1967) and made nine All-Star Teams (1957, 1959, 1961-64, 1966).[59] Bunning finished his career with a 224-184 record, 3.27 ERA, and 2,855 strikeouts. With such a long and impressive list of achievements, he was finally inducted into the Hall of Fame in 1996 by the Veterans Committee.

Bunning commanded four pitches: a slider, fastball, curve and change-up. His delivery was described as a "sweeping sidearm delivery." Ted Williams often remarked that his slider initially rose as it approached

---

59 "Jim Bunning," Baseball Reference: http://www.baseball-reference.com/players/b/bunniji01.shtml?redir. Retrieved on October 3, 2013.

the plate. Some accused him of throwing spitballs.[60] Allen Lewis recalled that Bunning was "the only pitcher I ever saw who never threw a pitch that he didn't know exactly what he was trying to do with it. He had purpose with every pitch."[61]

Although Bunning had already thrown a no-hitter versus the Boston Red Sox in 1958, his perfect game pitched on Father's Day is probably his most remembered achievement. Facing the Mets at Shea Stadium, Bunning was perfect through the first four innings, striking out 12 batters. Sensing something special was in the works, his manager made a series of defensive re-alignments, switching players with speed from infield to outfield positions. Bunning later told his teammates: "don't let anything drop." In the 5th inning, the cause was almost lost save for an outstanding play made by Phillies second baseman Tony Taylor. Jesse Gonder, catcher for the Mets, hit a hard line drive between first and second. Playing well toward second, Taylor was somehow able to knock the ball down with a diving play. Managing to then get to his knees quickly, he threw a bullet to first, just catching Gonder before he could reach the bag. Able to prevent any hits into the 9th inning, a calm and cool Bunning called his catcher out to the mound after getting the first batter. Instead of talking strategy or reviewing signals, he simply asked if he had any good jokes to help him relax. His catcher just laughed (thinking Bunning quite insane) and walked back to home. The final out was John Stephenson, a pinch-hitter, and Bunning got him with a nice slider. Pounding his glove in triumph, he was joined by teammates on the field in celebration. Not only was Bunning the first perfect game pitcher since 1922, he was the first National League pitcher since 1880 and just the fifth in baseball history.[62] At the time, Bunning had seven children. It must have been particularly sweet for him to achieve such a record on Father's Day. For a couple of years now, I have been collecting signed perfect game baseballs. My Jim Bunning signed ball is one of my favorites in the collection. The signature is clean, right in the sweet spot, the date clearly visible as is the accompanying P.G. It occupies a special place of honor in my own, diminutive hall of fame.

---

60 James and Neyer, Ibid., pp.150

61 "Jim Bunning," Baseball Hall of Fame: http://baseballhall.org/hof/Bunning-Jim. Retrieved on November 4, 2014.

62 Ralph Berger, "Jim Bunning" SABR: http://sabr.org/bioproj/person/bcacaa59. Retrieved on November 4, 2014.

While there is considerably less information on Bunning's perfect inning (as is all too common with immaculate innings), there are some recorded details. The game occurred on August the 2nd, 1959, with Bunning's Tigers playing against the Boston Red Sox at Briggs Stadium. Paul Foytack was the starting pitcher for the Tigers. By the top of the 9th inning, the Tigers were behind by one run, and Bunning was called in to replace Foytack. He did what needed to be done and then some. He struck out the side, retiring the bottom of the order in Sammy White (batting 7th), Jim Mahoney, and Ike Delock. Of the three, only Mahoney was caught looking at the third strike. Unfortunately for the Tigers, they could not produce any runs in the bottom of the 9th, losing to the Red Sox 5-4. There was no celebration on the mound for Bunning that day.

Bunning played his last game, for the Phillies, on September 3rd, 1971. Few ballplayers had quite the public life that Bunning had following his retirement from the game. A Republican politician, Bunning was an elected Member of the House of Representatives from Kentucky from 1987 to 1999 and then served as a United States Senator from 1999 to 2011. In 2001, the Phillies retired his number 14, forever enshrining his memory with the ball club.

Sandy Koufax
June 30th, 1962, April 19th, 1963 & April 18th, 1964

As a baseball fan, I sincerely regret never having had the chance to see Sandy Koufax pitch live. I have, of course, seen pictures and grainy video, which along with the many written descriptions of his style, is enough for me to know I missed something truly spectacular to behold. It seems only fitting then, that one of the game's greatest pitchers holds the distinction of being the only pitcher to record three immaculate innings, including back-to-back instances in '62 and '63. Even more impressive, Sandy Koufax did this in a career that was cut tragically short by injury. In this chapter we will review all three innings, even though they did not all occur in order.

Sanford Braun was born on the day before New Year's Eve in 1935 in Brooklyn, New York. Koufax was the name his mother took, following a second marriage that occurred when Sandy was just nine years old. He always regarded Irving Koufax as his father, not really knowing (or caring to know) Jack Braun, his biological father, all that well.

By all accounts, Koufax was a great athlete in high school; extremely competitive, strong and tall (6'2"), it was basketball, not baseball that was his first love. He did not seriously consider baseball until quite a bit latter in his youth. While attending the University of Cincinnati, he made the basketball team as a walk-on. By the spring of 1954 however, he was playing baseball for the varsity team, and it was there that he was first noticed by Dodgers' scout Bill Zinser. The scouting report Zinser made, for some reason, never made it to the front office. So at least for a time, Koufax was not on the Dodgers' radar. He eventually tried out for both the Giants and the Pirates. Indeed, Koufax very nearly became a Pirate, catching the eye and interest of then general manager of the club, Branch Rickey. Rickey said that he had the greatest arm he had ever seen; high praise from the baseball guru himself. Alas for Pirates fans, it was Rickey's son, Branch Jr., who convinced his father not to pursue Koufax.[63] In short time, he would sign a contract as a bonus baby with the Dodgers, a club he would pitch for throughout his entire career (his first appearance was on June 24th, 1955). The first five years of his career were difficult. He struggled with control and injuries and as a result, had his playing time reduced. No doubt this had something to do with being a 'bonus-baby.' Under the rules at the time, if a club signed a player under the bonus system, they had to keep him in the Majors for at least two seasons before it became an option to send him to the minors. Not only did Koufax come to the Dodgers with a big target on his back (a rookie with a big contract and no track record), he also missed the opportunity of refining and learning his craft in the minors. On this basis alone, it is remarkable that in just five years, he became the most dominating pitcher in the Majors. It is clear however, that Koufax was not entirely convinced he had the right stuff in those first few years. Not only did he enroll in evening classes in architecture at Columbia University, but he asked to be traded at the end of the 1960 season after he went 8-12. Koufax even considered quitting the game altogether, dropping everything to devote himself to an electronics business he had invested in earlier that same year. Thankfully, he was able to weather the storm and stay in the game.

Koufax was known for three pitches: a fastball, curve and change-up. His fastball in particular, was often a source of frustration for hitters for it appeared to rise just as it approached the plate.[64] This was largely due to Koufax having one of the most unique pitching styles of any player in baseball history. Conventionally, most pitchers use a three-quarter-arm motion, while a smaller number use a side-arm throwing action. Koufax used neither approach. His action involved an exaggerated over the top motion. His arm and body resembled a catapult. With a fully extended wind-up (and a high kicking action), Koufax literally propelled his arm

63 Jane Leavy, *Sandy Koufax: A Lefty's Legacy*, Perennial, 2010. pp. 54.

64 James and Neyer, Ibid. pp.270-271.

forward over the top to finish with his arm extended out toward home plate. It was not so much his arm that provided the power, but his legs and back. Regrettably, while this approach most certainly accounted for the great velocity he was able to get on his pitches, his technique did not allow for a lot of lateral movement in his delivery.

In thinking about his unusual pitching style, I am struck by the notion that regardless of his ability to get lateral movement, his success may have come from the fact that he was both a leftie and had a very unconventional arm-action. Studies on the kinematics (science of movement) of pitching and batting have repeatedly shown that skilled batters are successful not because they can see the ball coming, but because they can anticipate the flight or trajectory of the ball by attending to the position of the pitchers arm and wrist in space as he is winding up and about to release the ball.[65] There is a wonderful story about Jennie Finch, a former Olympian softball pitcher, who was able strike out All-Star players like Albert Pujols and Barry Bonds with a pitch that only topped out in the high 60 mph range.[66] It was puzzling to understand how she could have so much success facing the world's best batters when her pitch speed was well below the Major League average. The answer to the conundrum is found with Finch's arm action (coupled with the fact the mound in softball is only 40 feet from home plate). These great hitters were used to anticipating pitches following a three-quarter or side-arm position through space. They simply could not read her big, looping windmill action and therefore could not anticipate where the ball would be when it reached the plate. For the hitters Koufax faced, perhaps it was the same. His arm action was so unconventional, they had trouble reading the pre-release cues that good hitters rely upon. Couple this with Koufax's velocity, and you have a lethal combination. As Willie Mays once said, "I knew every pitch he was going to throw and still I couldn't hit him."[67] Mays might have known that a fastball was coming; he simply struggled to anticipate where because the usual cues he relied on were just not there.

65 See for example, Peter McLeod, "From Eye Movements to Actions: How Batsmen Hit the Ball," *Nature Neuroscience*, 2000, 3(12): 1340-45.

66 David Epstein, *The Sports Gene: Inside the Science of Extraordinary Athletic Performance.* Current, 2013, pp. 1-3.

67 Sandy Koufax and Ed Linn, *Koufax*, New York: Viking Press, 1966, pp. 153.

Koufax's career numbers require no accompanying commentary. He played twelve seasons, and recorded an astonishing 165-87 record. Over his career, the Dodger ace accumulated a 2.76 ERA, 2,396 strikeouts, six All-Star appearances (1961-62, 1963-65), three Cy Young awards (1963, 1965, 1966), three pitching Triple Crowns (1963, 1965, 1966) and two World Series MVPs (1963, 1965). Koufax pitched four no-hitters and a perfect game in 1965. Inducted into the Hall of Fame on the first ballot in 1972, with 86.87% of the vote, he was named to the MLB All-Century Team and the MLB All-Time Team.

All three of Koufax's perfect innings (and his no-hitters and perfect game for that matter) came at the height of the '61-'66 period that is often referred to simply as 'Koufax's Domination.' For example, in the second part of that era, from '63 to '66, he recorded 97 wins and 27 losses. His ERA per season during this time was 1.88, 1.74, 2.04, and 1.73. [68]

His first perfect inning occurred in the top of the 1st in a game pitting the Dodgers against the New York Mets on June 30th, 1962. Koufax struck out the side consisting of Richie Ashburn, Rod Kanehl and Félix Mantilla on nine pitches. The first and second batters struck out swinging, while Mantilla was caught looking at strike three. This game was also one of Koufax's four no-hitters: he finished the game having pitched 9 innings with no hits, no runs and just 5 walked batters. The Dodgers won that day at home, 5-0.

The second immaculate inning occurred the following season on April 19th, 1963. This was only the second time a pitcher had recorded consecutive immaculate innings, and more than thirty years since Grove had initially achieved the distinction. Facing the Houston Colt .45s at Dodger Stadium, Koufax took the mound at the top of the 5th to face the bottom of their lineup: Bob Aspromonte, Jim Campbell and Turk Farrell. Once again, all three were quickly dispatched: Aspromonte swinging, Campbell looking and Farrell swinging. Koufax finished with a complete game win (2-0), allowing just 2 hits, 2 walks and striking out 14 batters. Overall, his record improved to 2-1 early in the '63 season.

The final immaculate inning in Koufax's career came on April 18th, 1964 in a game against the Cincinnati Reds. At Dodger Stadium once again, Koufax struck out Leo Cárdenas swinging, Johnny Edwards look-

---

68 Benjamin G. Rader, *Baseball. A History of America's Game.* 3rd Edition. University of
   Illinois Press, 2008. pp. 185.

ing and finally, Jim Maloney swinging in the 3rd. Though scoreless at this point in the game, a home run by the Reds' Deron Johnson in the 4th added 3 runs. In the 8th, Wally Moon pinch-hit for Koufax, but he and the middle of the Dodgers order could not rally and they ended up losing 3-0. Koufax was tagged with the loss, pitching 8 innings and allowing 3 runs off 3 hits.

Before concluding, it is important to discuss two significant off-field events that are essential parts of the overall Koufax story. The first key event was Koufax's decision to not pitch in the opening game of the 1965 World Series because it fell on Yom Kippur. Although already a celebrity in the Jewish community, especially in Brooklyn, Koufax's decision to follow his personal beliefs instead of his professional obligations forever solidified his status as a superstar among Jewish fans.[69]

The second event was Koufax and Dodger teammate Don Drysdale's double contract holdout in 1966.[70] Recognizing that Dodger General Manager, Buzzie Bavasi, was attempting to play one star off the other during contract negotiations, the two decided to break with tradition and negotiate as a duo. Of course, there was no mechanism for collective bargaining in Major League Baseball at that time, and players were still bound by the reserve clause. In the drama that unfolded, which saw both stars taking time off to appear in a movie and a nasty public relations campaign by management to smear their good names, both ended up settling and rejoining the team before the regular season commenced. [71] Bavasi wrote about the incident in *Sports Illustrated* the following year, remarking "To tell the truth, I wasn't too successful in the famous Koufax-Drysdale double holdout in 1966. I mean, when the smoke cleared they stood together on the battlefield with $235,000 between them, and I stood there with a blood-stained cashbox."[72]

Aside from these key events, another standout part of the Koufax story was his rapidly declining health as his career progressed. There are some truly disturbing stories about Koufax playing through incredible pain in his final two seasons. His left arm was described as being entirely black and blue from hemorrhaging. Post-game rituals routinely included immers-

69 Jane Leavy. Opt Cit. pp.168-171.

70 Benjamin G. Rader. Opt Cit. pp. 207.

71 Jane Leavy, Opt Cit. pp. 204-211.

72 Buzzie Bavasi. "The Great Holdout," *Sports Illustrated*. (May 15, 1967) reprinted in: http://www.si.com/vault/1967/05/15/610695/the-great-holdout

ing his arm in an ice-bath for hours. As the pain worsened, Koufax also increasingly relied on a host of new, very powerful drugs. In the end, facing the threat of permanent disability from the traumatic arthritis that affected his left elbow, Koufax retired from baseball at the age of 30.[73] He pitched his final game on October 2nd, 1966. At the press conference announcing his retirement that year, he said: "I've had a few too many shots and taken a few too many pills. ... I had to take a shot every ballgame. That's more than I wanted to do. I had stomachaches from the pain pills. I'd be high half the time in ballgames from the pills. I don't want that."[74]

73 "Sandy Koufax Hall of Fame Page," Baseball Hall of Fame: http://baseballhall.org/hof/koufax-sandy. Retrieved on November 7, 2014.

74 "Sandy Koufax on Pitching and Pain," LA Times. (April 10, 1969), reprinted in: http://latimesblogs.latimes.com/thedailymirror/2009/04/april-10-1969--sandy-koufax-talked-about-a-subject-he-knew-too-well--pain--arms-werent-made-to-do-what-pitchers-are-asked-t.html. Retrieved on November 8, 2014.

Tony Cloninger
June 15th, 1963

Sandwiched between Koufax's back-to-back perfect innings in 1963 and '64 is the second perfect inning pitched in '63; the pitcher in question was Tony Cloninger. Born in Lincoln County, North Carolina on August 13th, 1940, while most of Western Europe was entrenched in the Second World War, Tony Lee Cloninger came into the world, destined to become a big league pitcher. Cloninger came from a family with baseball in their DNA: he had an older brother who turned down offers to play professionally, and two sons who became pro ballplayers in the 1980s.[75] While he began his playing career as a catcher, his coaches would eventually take note of his strong arm and move the young lad from behind the plate to the top of the mound.

In a career spanning twelve seasons, Cloninger played for three different Major League clubs: the Milwaukee/Atlanta Braves (1961-68), Cincinnati Reds (1968-1971) and St. Louis Cardinals (1972). A right-handed power pitcher, Cloninger was known to have three pitches, a fastball, change-up and curve ball.[76] He made his Major League debut with the Braves on June 15th, 1961. Statistically, his best season came with the Braves in '65 when he finished with a career-high 24 wins, 211 strikeouts, and a 3.29 ERA.

---

75 David E. Skelton, "Tony Cloninger," SABR: http://sabr.org/bioproj/person/76a4cb2f. Retrieved on October 5, 2014.

76 James and Neyer, Ibid, pp. 167.

Cloninger ended his career with a 113-97 record, 1,120 strikeouts, and a 4.07 ERA over 1,767.2 innings.

Cloninger was no slouch at the plate either. A right-handed hitter, his career .192 AVG, 67 RBIs and 11 homers is a batting line any pitcher would be proud to have on their stat sheet. In 1966 alone, the power pitcher hit 5 home runs, including 2 grand slam homers in a game against the Giants at Candlestick Park, a game the Braves won 17-3. To date, he is the only pitcher in history to hit 2 grand slams in a single game and one of only three pitchers in history—along with Don Newcombe and Rick Wise— to hit 2 home runs in a single game.[77] Cloninger would later admit that part of his hitting success was due to the tutelage he received from Eddie Mathews and Hank Aaron.[78]

On June 15th, 1963, Cloninger added a perfect inning to his list of unique achievements. Facing the Philadelphia Phillies in the top of the 8th inning, he struck out centre fielder Tony González, who was pinch-hitting for the catcher Earl Averill batting in the number 6 spot, before pinch-hitter Clay Dalrymple, and shortstop Rubén Amaro met the same fate. Cloninger, pitching in relief of starter Denny Lemaster that day, received the win; pitching 4.2 innings, allowing just 3 hits, no earned runs, 1 walk and 8 strikeouts. The Braves beat the Phillies, 5-3.

Not only did Cloninger pitch for the Braves in 1965, he was also the opening day pitcher for the controversial 1966 season when the team relocated to Atlanta. During the '65 season, Cloninger and his teammates played amidst court cases, injunctions and appeals, along with the escalating hostility of the fan base toward ownership. Though Milwaukee fans were likely less shocked than Bostonians were when their team of 82 years left for their minor-league affiliate, the move still left a bad taste. Much of this anger stemmed from the fact that ownership argued a move was necessary due to dwindling fan support. Playing in this volatile climate, it is hardly surprising that the Braves players were happy just to get out that city. Years after the fact, Cloninger would admit: "I was excited about going to Atlanta, about being able to pitch not too far from my North Carolina home."[79] However, his opening day performance in his new home was not

---

77 Skelton, Ibid.

78 Wilt Browning, "Tony Cloniger" North Carolina Sports Hall of Fame: http://www. ncshof.org/2012/03/09/tony-cloninger/. Retrieved on October 5, 2014.

79 Browing, Ibid.

positive. A 13-inning loss, it proved to be a harbinger for a season that was far from his best. Cloninger eventually left Atlanta for Cincinnati in 1968. He would stay with the Reds until 1971, before finishing his career in St. Louis in the '72 season.

In 1988, Cloninger returned to professional baseball, beginning as a pitching coach with the Albany-Colonie Yankees of the Eastern League before serving as a bullpen coach for the Yankees under both Buck Showalter and Joe Torre. With Torre's powerhouse team, he was part of four World Series championships; first in 1996, then again from 1998 to 2000. After a brief hiatus, he returned to coach with the Red Sox from 2002-2003. In 2004, he was inducted to the North Carolina Sports Hall of Fame.

Bob Bruce
April 19th 1964

Just one day after Koufax pitched his third immaculate inning, Bob Bruce recorded his perfect inning in a game against the St. Louis Cardinals. Robert James Bruce was born in Detroit, Michigan on May 16th, 1933. A right-handed pitcher who also batted right, he made his debut on September 14th, 1959 for his hometown Tigers. He would only play three seasons with the Tigers, however, before being traded to the new expansion franchise, the Houston Colt .45s. In their inaugural season in 1962, Bruce was one of the premiere players, along with fellow pitcher Turk Farrell. In the first few years of the new club, he became the first pitcher to win 15 games for Houston in 1964. From 1962 to 66, Bruce would pitch for the .45s. His last appearance in the Majors was on the June 24th, 1967 as a member of the Atlanta Braves. Over nine seasons in the Majors, he had a record of 49-71, 3.85 ERA and 733 strikeouts.

Although professional baseball had been played in Houston since 1888 (the minor league Houston Buffaloes played there from 1888 to 1961), it was not until 1962 that Houston became home to a new team as part of the National League expansion. William Neder is credited with coming up with the team name (he won a contest held by the new owners prior to the start of the '62 season). The reference to the gun that had "won the West" was no doubt well-received by local fans, and was befitting of the new influence the West was having in America, both economically in general and in baseball specifically. Starting in 1958 when the Dodgers left Brooklyn for Los Angeles, clubs struggling in their current markets moved West to places like Atlanta (1966) and Arlington, Texas (1972). At the same time, new franchises were created in Los Angeles (Angels, 1961), Kansas City (Royals, 1969), San Diego (Padres, 1969) and Seattle (Pilots, 1969). Outside of Houston, many readers will not be familiar with the name Colt .45s. It was not until the team moved to the Astrodome in 1965 that the current team name, the Houston Astros, was finally adopted. Bruce was around not only for the team's inaugural season, but he also pitched in the world's first domed sports stadium.

On April 19th, 1964, Bob Bruce started the 8th inning in relief of Jim Beauchamp (who had come into the game pinch hitting for starter Don Nottebart in the 7th) with the Cardinals already ahead by 5 runs. Facing the heart of the line-up, Bruce retired Bill White, Charlie James and Ken Boyer on nine strikes. James was left looking at the last strike, while White and Boyer both struck out swinging. Bruce finished the day, giving up a single in the top half of the 9th, before striking out the next three batters again. But for one swing, he might have been able to record back-to-back perfect innings in the same game, a feat that has yet to be achieved by any Major League pitcher. The Colt .45s lost the game, 6-1.

Beyond his membership in this fraternity, there is little else of note to say about Bob Bruce. At the time of writing of this book, he was 81 years old. Like so many of his brethren, he is among the many whose professional baseball careers are now but brief entries and footnotes in record books and online sources.

Al Downing
August 11th, 1967

Fully three years would pass before the next immaculate inning occurred. This time, the pitcher was Al Downing. Born in Trenton, New Jersey on June 28th, 1941, Alphonso Erwin Downing spent the first nine seasons of his career with the New York Yankees (1961-1969), followed by Oakland and Milwaukee in 1970, and then the final seven with the Los Angeles Dodgers (1971-1977). In 1961, having only just signed as an amateur free agent with the Yanks, Downing made the Major League roster in July of that same year. Two seasons later in 1963, a year the Bronx Bombers would sweep the Los Angeles Dodgers in the World Series, Downing went 13 and 5 with a 2.56 ERA in just his first full season with the team. The following year, he would win 13 games, lose 8, and led the league in strikeouts with 217. Overall, his career stats are consistent with his impressive start to a long career in the Majors: a win-loss record of 123 to 107, a career ERA of 3.22, and 1,639 strikeouts.

In addition to his perfect inning, there are three especially noteworthy achievements to Downing's career. In 1967, he represented the Yankees at the All-Star Game during a season where he went 14-10. In 1970, Downing was on the move, first with an offseason trade to the Oakland A's and then a midseason trade to Milwaukee. The quick moves did little for his game, and he finished that season with a losing record of 2-10 (Downing's performance, despite a 3.34 ERA, was relatively consistent with a Brewer's club that only narrowly averted 100 losses). In the off-season, he was once again traded, this time to the Dodgers. By the numbers, moving to the National League was just what Downing needed, as he won 20 games with 5 shutouts. Although he finished third behind Tom Seaver and Fergie Jenkins in the '71 Cy Young Award race, he still received the National League Comeback Player of the Year Award.

The final thing Downing will be remembered for was his role in the single biggest sporting moment of 1974, and indeed a moment of historical import for all of baseball—Hank Aaron's record breaking 715th home run on April 8th. The context of this event cannot be minimized. First, it is fair to say that baseball in the early 1970s was in trouble. Attendance was on the decline, and baseball was experimenting (both individual clubs and the league as a whole) with changes to the game that would re-ignite fan passion and hold-off the charge of America's increasing love affair with football. Aaron's run at Babe Ruth's record did much to propel baseball back into the forefront of American popular culture. Yet it came at a high personal cost for Aaron, who had to endure hate mail, vicious taunting and death threats. Though nearly one-third of all players in baseball were black by 1975, and integration of the league with Jackie Robinson in 1947 seemed like a lifetime away, racism was still an extremely troubling issue in a country emerging from the shadow of Jim Crow-era segregation. [80]

Some forty years after the historic event, during a celebration of the achievement held at the New York Baseball Writers' Association of America dinner in 2014, the two would be reunited once more. With his arm around Downing, Aaron commented that not enough had been said about him, "He was a great pitcher." The pitch that Aaron hit was a sinker, which according to Downing, "didn't sink". Both laughing, Aaron added: "I was trying to hit before it sank, but it didn't sink." [81]

As I noted in the first chapter, about a third of all perfect innings occur late in the game, especially in the modern era; however, on August 11th, 1967, Downing defied that tendency, striking out Tony Horton (the number four batter in the lineup), Don Demeter and Duke Sims on nine pitches

---

80 Bob Nightengale, "Number of African-American baseball players dips again," *USA Today* (April16, 2012) as reprinted in http://usatoday30.usatoday.com/sports/baseball/story/2012-04-15/baseball-jackie-robinson/54302108/1 _Viewed August 3rd, 2014.

81 "Hank Aaron and Al Downing remember home run No. 715," MLB.COM: https://www.youtube.com/watch?v=quNhp49A6J0. Viewed on August 3, 2014.

in the 2nd inning. Facing the Indians in Cleveland, the Yankees would go on to win that game, 5-3. Downing would pitch all 9 innings, striking out 12 batters, allowing 2 earned runs (and two home runs) off 8 hits, while issuing 2 walks.

Downing continued in baseball as a colour commentator for the Dodgers' cable TV broadcasts through most of the 1980s, and as a radio broadcaster for CBS Radio in the following decade. At the time of writing, he was 73.

Nolan Ryan
April 19th, 1968 & July 9th, 1972

If pitching an immaculate inning is remarkably rare, pitching more than one is astoundingly improbable. Lynn Nolan Ryan Jr. is one of only four pitchers to achieve this improbability, along with Lefty Grove, Sandy Koufax (both already discussed) and Randy Johnson. With the difficulty of repeating such a rare feat of mastery being extremely high, it is no wonder that the four who have done so are four of the greatest pitchers in the game's history.

Ryan was born in Refugio, Texas on January 31st, 1947. The youngest in a family of six children, Ryan began his pitching career in Alvin Texas Little League Baseball at the age of nine. By the time he was 11 he was a Little League All-Star, and before his 16th birthday he had recorded his first no-hitter.[82] Drafted by the New York Mets in the twelve round of the amateur draft in 1965, he made his Major League debut on September 11th, 1966, for the Mets, making him the second youngest player to play in the Majors.

Over his career, one that lasted for a record breaking twenty-seven years, Ryan played for four different clubs: the New York Mets (1966, 1968-71), California Angels (1972-79), Houston Astros (1980-88) and the Texas Rangers (1989-1993). Over that time, he compiled an incredible list of achievements and records; however, not all of these achievements are

---

82 Sanna, Ellyn, *Nolan Ryan.* The Rosen Publishing Group.

necessarily prized among pitchers. For example, his career win-loss record of 324-292 is far from the records achieved from most other Hall of Fame pitchers. Yet, this is precisely the record that others have used to illustrate the problems with evaluating pitchers on the basis of wins and losses alone.[83] His record is more a reflection of the caliber of teams on which Ryan played than his personal performance: win-loss after all is a team statistic, not an individual player stat. Over his career, Ryan compiled 5,714 strikeouts the most ever in the history of baseball by a sizeable margin (839 more than second-place Randy Johnson). Impressive indeed, but he also holds the all-time record for walks, again by a sizeable margin (962) over second-place Steve Carlton. Without any caveats however, here are some of the Nolan's most notable achievements: he was an eight-time All-Star (1972, 1973, 1975, 1977, 1979, 1981, 1985 and 1989), a two-time National League ERA champion (1981, 1987), and a twelve-time strikeout champion (1972-74, 1976-79, 1987-1991). Remarkably, he has pitched a total of 7 career no-hitters. Nolan's number has been retired by three of the four clubs he played with, making him the only pitcher and the only baseball player other than Jackie Robinson to have his number retired by more than one ball club. He was inducted into the Hall of Fame in 1999 with more than 98% of the total votes on the first ballot.

Ryan's first immaculate inning occurred on April 19th, 1968: a game that pitted his Mets against the Los Angeles Dodgers at Shea Stadium. Ryan was hot out of the gate, striking out the top of the order in the 1st. After a rocky 2nd, Ryan faced the number nine batter and the top of the order in the top of the 3rd, striking out all three (Claude Osteen, Wes Parker and Zoilo Versalles) on nine pitches. Protecting a slim 1-run lead in the 7th, Ryan surrendered a home run to Dodgers catcher Tom Haller before finally ending the inning. In the top of the 8th Ryan again took the mound, but was replaced by Bill Short after giving up a one-out single. With a man on base, and two outs, Lefebvre doubled off of Short to score a run. One more run would score before the end of the inning, and the Dodgers took a 3-1 lead into the bottom of the 8th inning. Although the Mets would get a run back in the 9th, they lost that day, 3-2. For Ryan's part, he went 7.1 innings, allowing 2 runs on 6 hits and 4 walks, but striking out 11 batters.

---

83 Keith Woolner and Dayn Perry, "Why are pitchers so unpredictable?" *Baseball Between the Numbers- Why Everything You Know about the Game is Wrong*. Jonah Keri ed. Perseus Books Group, New York, pp. 51.

It would be four more years before Ryan achieved his second immaculate inning. This time playing for the Angels, Ryan took the mound facing the Red Sox at Anaheim Stadium on July 9th, 1972. In the top of the 3rd, facing the number six batter, Carlton Fisk, and the 7th and 8th hitters in Bob Burda and Juan Beníquez, Ryan threw nine pitches to strikeout all three men. Burda was caught looking, while Fisk and Beníquez were clean strikeouts. Ryan finished the game that day with a shutout, allowing just 1 hit, 1 walk and 16 strikeouts, improving his record to 11-5 for the season. The win helped an otherwise mediocre Angels team, as they improved to 35-42.

There are two images of Ryan that stick out in my mind. Both are violent, which is in contrast to the sometimes peaceful, even pastoral image that baseball conjures. The first involves a young Bo Jackson, back in 1990. Playing for Kansas City at the time, Jackson hit a line drive right at Ryan, catching him in the face. Blood streaming from his lip onto his white jersey, Ryan looked around for the ball, found it, and threw it to first in time to get the out. Ryan refused to leave the game. The image of the blood-soaked warrior has been immortalized in memorabilia and imprinted in the minds of those who have seen the event (YouTube footage is available also if you are so inclined).[84]

The second involved a duel between Chicago White Sox, Robin Ventura and Ryan while he played for the Rangers. On August 4th, 1993, in the top of the 3rd, Ryan plugged Ventura in the ribs, with the smack allegedly being clearly audible throughout the stadium. Though it initially seemed as if Ventura would just take his base, he suddenly threw down his bat and helmet and charged the mound. A twenty-year age difference notwithstanding, without hesitation Ryan stepped down off the mound to meet Ventura, immediately putting him in a head-lock before delivering several blows to his skull. As the one-sided fight occurred, the benches cleared and the two were separated in the ensuing melee. Just when it seemed that the fighting was over, a second fight broke out (interestingly, once again involving Bo Jackson). When everyone was finally separated, Rangers' Nicky Hatcher had a visible cut over his right eye. Eventually both teams returned to the dugout amid chants of "Nolan, Nolan."

---

84 Dakota Gardner, "5 moments when Nolan Ryan was the baddest man in baseball," MLB.com: http://wapc.mlb.com/cutfour/2014/01/31/67126650/video-nolan-ryan-birthday-best-performance. Retrieved on December 2, 2014.

After his retirement from the Majors, Ryan continued to be actively involved in baseball with his old club the Rangers. Beginning first as President in 2008, Ryan and Chuck Greenberg eventually joined forces to purchase the club in 2010. Ryan later became CEO of the organization, a position he held until 2013 when he stepped down. Currently, he works as an executive advisor to the other team in Texas he played for, the Houston Astros.

Bob Gibson
May 12th, 1969

The last pitcher to record an immaculate inning in the 1960s was pitching legend Bob Gibson. Born in Omaha, Nebraska on November 9th, 1935, Robert "Bob" Gibson was a right-handed starting pitcher, who played seventeen seasons with the St. Louis Cardinals (1959-1975). Signed as an amateur free agent by the Cards in 1957, "Gibby" or "Hoot", as he was nicknamed, made his first appearance for the Red Birds on April 15th, 1959. Gibson threw five pitches: a rising fastball, slider, sinking fastball, curve and change-up. By his own account, he felt short-changed by the scouting report and added four pitches to his arsenal: a brush-back, a hit-batsman and two additional pitches, a fastball and curve, that did come with any distinguishing adjectives.[85] As a pitcher, Hoot was intense, tough and very competitive. There are many stories in evidence of this—Jim Hart's broken shoulder, a reward for crowding the plate is one example.[86] According to Gibson though: "I'd like to think that the term 'intensity' comes much closer to summarizing my pitching style than do qualities like meanness and anger, which were merely devices."[87]

---

85 James and Neyer, Op Cit. pp.217.

86 Bob Gibson with Lonnie Wheeler, *Stranger To The Game: The Autobiography of Bob Gibson*, New York: Penguin Books, 1994, pp.76.

87 Gibson and Wheel, Ibid, pp.166-67.

His career record is truly something to behold, with a 251-174 record, 2.91 ERA, 1.188 WHIP (walks plus hits per inning pitched) and 3,117 strikeouts over 528 games and 3,884.1 innings. He holds six different pitching records: most consecutive quality starts—26; most consecutive starts with 6 or more innings pitched—78; the National League Shutout Championships in the Live-ball Era—led or tied four times; Gold Glove for Pitchers—9 consecutive times, ranking him third among pitchers all-time; lowest single season ERA, 1.12 in 1968; and most strikeouts in a World Series Game (see below). He was a nine-time All-Star (1962(2x), 1965-1970, 1972), played on two World Series teams (1964 and 1967), was MVP for the National League in 1968, a two-time Cy Young winner (1968, 1970) and World Series MVP twice (1964 and 1967).

Gibson's immaculate inning occurred on May 12th, 1969 in the 7th inning of a game against the Los Angeles Dodgers. To that point, Gibson had held the Dodgers to just one run. To start the 7th, he struck out Gabrielson on 3 pitches. Number eight batter Paul Popovich followed and struck out on 3 pitches. Pinch hitter John Miller then closed the inning by striking out looking. Gibson would finish the game, getting the win with just 2 earned runs off 7 hits, walking 2 and striking out 6 batters. The final score was 6-2.

Gibson was a big part of how 1968 came to be known as the "year of the pitcher." That year, Gibson pitched in more than 300 innings and recorded an ERA of 1.12. His ERA was the lowest in the Majors since Dutch Leonard posted a .96 ERA in 1914.[88] He also threw 13 shutouts that season and held opposing hitters to a .184 average, with an overall record of 22-9. More impressive feats came in the post season. In Game One of the '68 World Series against the Tigers, Gibson struck out 17 batters, setting a new record for strikeouts in a single World Series game (the previous record of 15 was held by none other than Sandy Koufax). The domination of pitchers that season, especially Gibson, forced a number of rule changes for the 1969 season. The pitcher's mound was lowered by 5" and the strike zone was reduced from the armpit of the batter to the jersey letters. Not surprisingly, both of these changes are referred to as the "Gibson rules."[89]

---

88 "Bob Gibson Player Page," Op cit.

89 Feldmann, Doug, *Gibson's Last Stand: The Rise, Fall, and Near Misses of the St. Louis Cardinals, 1969–1975*. Columbia: University of Missouri Press, 2011, spp. 2.

Gibson's greatness as a pitcher is undeniable, but like many of the pitchers in this collection, baseball was not his only sport, or even his favourite, when he was growing up. It was basketball, not baseball, that was Gibson's passion and he played the game while attending high school in Omaha. It would also appear he had talent for track and field. While attending Omaha Technical High School, he set the record for high jump. Later, he attended Creighton University, where he majored in sociology, played basketball and "minored" in baseball.[90] Of course, in a few short years, that would all change.

Bob Gibson played his final game for the Cardinals on September 3rd, 1975. In 1981, he was inducted into the Hall of Fame on the first ballot, capturing 84% of the vote. After baseball, Gibson spent time as a pitching coach, first with the Braves (1982) and later with the Cardinals (1995). Both times he coached under Joe Torre, and both times he left when Joe left.[91] He was 78 when this chapter was written and still living in Omaha.

---

90 Terry Sloope, "Bob Gibson," SABR: http://sabr.org/bioproj/person/34500d95#sdendnote3sym. Retrieved on November 8th, 2014.

91 Sloope, Op Cit.

PART III: 1970-1989

Bill Wilson
July 6th, 1971

The 1970s were an interesting time in Major League Baseball. Some have described it as the decade of the player, citing the institution of free agency and arbitration, and the beginning of a shift from chattel status (the product of the reserve clause) to emancipated professional. Indeed, players' salaries rose by more than 400%. The average salary of a ball player in 1970 was $29,000 and by the end of the decade it was $146,000.[92] The game itself was also changing. By the early '70s, America's love affair with the national pastime was showing signs of fading. Football, brash and aggressive, was on the rise and threatening the slower, more pastoral game of baseball. In response, the designated hitter (DH) became part of the batting lineup in the American League in 1973—a direct response to the domination of pitching that had come to define the game in the late 1960s. The formula was more offense equals more excitement. Uniforms were bolder and more colorful (think about the Oakland A's green and gold and the Houston Astros' rainbow). Players, reflecting the fashion of the time, suddenly seemed a whole lot less conservative, relative to the crew cut, clean-shaven look of the previous eras. Again, the A's were a standout here: muttonchops and long hair all became part of the look that defined

---

92 Benjamin Rader, *Baseball: A History of America's Game*, 3rd Edition. University of Illnois Press, 2008. pp. 213.

this period. In Matthew Silverman's book *Swinging '73*, we are reminded of what was arguably the most exciting and strange year of that decade in baseball.[93] In that inaugural year of the DH, fans also said goodbye to Willie Mays, and read with titillation, stories of wife-swapping Yankee pitchers (free love still in vogue). It was also the year of the improbable rise of the Mets and the domination of the A's, who won their second of what was to be three World Series championships, back to back, that decade. The A's, the Cincinnati Reds and the Yankees would dominate the Majors during this time. Catfish Hunter, Pete Rose, Johnny Bench, and 'Mr. October' Reggie Jackson embodied the spirit of the time and quickly became the faces of the game. Flamboyant, brash, tough, and unique are all adjectives that come to mind when we think of those players. Amidst the backdrop of all that, there were eight immaculate innings pitched that decade by eight different pitchers: three of those happened in 1971. The first to record the feat was Bill Wilson.

Bill Harlan Wilson was born on September 21st, 1942, in Pomery, Ohio. His career in the Majors was short, lasting only five, sometimes incomplete, seasons. A right-handed reliever, he played for just one club, the Phillies from 1969 to 1973. He was signed as an amateur free agent in 1961, but did not make his first appearance until April 8th, 1971.[94] Bill was known for one pitch, his slider. One scouting report noted his control, recommending him as a possible reliever, also describing his slider as good.[95] His last appearance was for the Phillies on September 26th, 1973. He had a career win-loss record of 9-15, an ERA of 4.22 and 171 strikeouts over 179 games.

On July 6th, 1971, the Phillies played the Atlanta Braves at Atlanta Stadium in an evening contest. Wilson came into the game in relief of Bobby Pfeil in the bottom of the 7th to face the top of the order, his club behind 5-2. He was able to induce a lineout, groundout and pop fly, giving his team a chance in the 8th to close the gap. The Phillies did not capitalize and Wilson returned in the bottom of the inning to face the 4th, 5th and 6th hitters in the lineup that day for the Braves: Darrell Evans, Hal King, and Earl Williams. He retired the side on nine pitches, all three struck

---

93 Matthew Silverman, *Swinging '73. Baseball Wildest Season.* Lyons Press, 2013. pp. 15-40.

94 "Bill Wilson Player Page," Baseball Reference: http://www.baseball-reference.com/players/w/wilsobi03.shtml. Retrieved November 7, 2014.

95 James and Neyer, Op Cit., pp. 429.

out swinging. The Phillies had one more chance. With two strikeouts, the leadoff hitter, Terry Harmon (second base) was able to draw a walk off George Stone. Next up, Larry Bowa (shortstop) hit a single past 3rd base, advancing Harmon to second. Sensing a breakdown, manager Lum Harris pulled Stone and went to Cecil Upshaw. On the next batter, Harmon and Bowa both moved up one base on a passed ball to left fielder Don Money. Upshaw then proceeded to load the bases by walking Money. As exciting as the rally was however, it came to an end when the number four hitter, Deron Johnson (first base), lined out to right field to end the inning and the ball game. Wilson pitched 2 innings, allowing no hits or walks. The Braves won any way, 5-2.

Every once and awhile, unusual circumstances occur in a game. For example, when there is an ejection of position players or multiple injuries, the resulting holes in the infield leave a pitcher as the manager's only option to plug the gaps. After all, the bullpen is large, and there are only so many players on the bench. Beyond his immaculate inning, historians of the game may well remember that Bill Wilson was called on for such role, playing third base in the 8th inning on August 6th, 1971. With one out in the bottom of the inning, Phillies manager Frank Lucchesi called for a different reliever to come in and face Willie Stargell. Rather than pull Wilson from the game altogether though, he opted to move Bill to third. Left-handed pitcher Terry Harmon then replaced Joe Hoerner, the Phillies regular third baseman. Harmon would stay in for one out, after which infielder Bobby Pfiel was called into to play third, and Wilson returned to the mound, pitching till the end of the game. According to Philippe Cousineau, there are three reasons why a Major League pitcher might be called upon to play multiple positions in a game: (1) the manager has run out of players; (2) the manager is playing a specific strategy, the so-called pitcher in the outfield move; and (3) to indulge a favourite son.[96] In this instance, it would seem as though the second explanation was at play. Lucchesi wanted to keep Wilson in the game (clearly he was pitching well), but preferred the lefty match-up against Stargell. Given that the Phillies won and Harmon got the out, the skipper made the right call. What is noteworthy here is that

96 Philippe Cousineau, "Pitchers in the Field: The Use of Pitchers at Other Positions in the Major Leagues, 1969–2009," *Baseball Research Journal* (Fall, 2011): http://sabr. org/research/pitchers-field-use-pitchers-other-positions-major-leagues-1969-2009. Retrieved on September 16, 2014.

it is far more common to move a pitcher to the outfield. Very few pitchers have played infield and pitched in the same game. Wilson was the last pitcher for the Phillies to play a different position until Roy Oswalt left the bullpen to play left field in a game against the Houston Astros in 2010. Other than that, there is simply not much to say about Bill Wilson's career. He died far too young at age 50, while living in Broken Arrow, Oklahoma.

John Strohmayer
July 10th, 1971

John Emery Strohmayer was born on October 13th, 1946, in Belle Foruche, South Dakota. He was the eighteenth pitcher in Major League history to pitch an immaculate inning, and he did so wearing that iconic, and very '70s, Expos logo. Originally drafted by the Oakland A's in 1968, he would not make his Major League debut until April 29th, 1970, and by that time, he was playing for the Expos. He stayed with Montreal for three seasons, until he was claimed off waivers by the Mets in July, 1973. (He joined the Mets at exactly the time they made that memorable and highly improbable run to the World Series, ultimately losing to the A's in October). His final appearance in the Majors came in September, 1974. Strohmayer retired after a shoulder injury, finishing with a career 11-9 record, 4.47 ERA, and 200 strikeouts.

On July 10th, 1971, the Expos were in Philadelphia, playing the first game of a double-header between the clubs. In the bottom of the 5th, Strohmayer took the mound to face the 8th and 9th batters in the line-up, and the lead-off hitter—Mike Ryan, Woodie Fryman, and Denny Doyle. Strohmayer would retire them in order, catching Fryman looking at strike three, and Ryan and Doyle swinging away. Strohmayer however, would not come out on top that day. Taking the loss (final score, 2-0), he pitched 7 innings, allowing 2 runs off 4 hits. Coming into this game, neither club was having a good season—both playing well below .500.

Outside of professional ball, Strohmayer had many significant, personal achievements. Prior to his career in the Majors, Strohmayer played for the Pacific Tigers, at the University of the Pacific in Stockton, California until 1968 (fans today might recognize another famous alum of that school, Chase Headley). In 1990, he was inducted into their Hall of Fame.[97] After he left the Majors, he returned to university to complete a degree in education. Following this was a successful thirty-two year career in that profession, including becoming Superintendent of the Gateway Unified School District in Redding, California in 2002. He retired in 2009, the same year he and fifteen other employees of that school district won a $76 million lottery[98]. His retirement from education, however, had more to do with poor health than with new-found wealth. Interesting to contemplate whether a donation of $76 million toward the creation of a new park in Montreal would have changed the Expos fortunes in '04. When one examines the events and actions of the key players (the owners, Bud Selig, and local government) surrounding that period though, I am doubtful.

---

97 "Pacific Athletics Hall of Fame," Pacific Tigers: http://www.pacifictigers.com/ information/hall_of_fame/all_time/index. Retrieved on August 15, 2014.

98 Rob Rogers, "Gateway schools superintendent retires after 32 years," *Record* Searchlight (Feb. 18, 2009): http://www.redding.com/news/gateway-schools-superintendent-retires-after-32. Retrieved August 15, 2014.

Milt Pappas
September 24th, 1971

Milt Pappas was born Miltiades Stergios Papastergios, on May 11th, 1939. Another baseball great born in the 'Motor City' of Detroit, Milt pitched a successful seventeen-year career in the Majors for four different clubs from 1957 to 1973: the Baltimore Orioles (1957-65), the Reds (1966-68), the Braves (1968-70), and the Cubs (1970-73). Signed directly out of high school, Pappas pitched his first game for the Orioles on August 10th, 1957, at the age of 18.

Pappas has one of the more memorable nicknames in Major League baseball. While dubbed "Gimpy" which, according to Milt, happened when he was 17 following a knee operation, it certainly did not describe his physical appearance or ability.[99] Noted for his control, Pappas had impressive numbers for someone not part of the Cooperstown elite. Over his career, he started 465 out of the 520 games he played, recorded a 209-164 record, 43 shutouts, 1,728 strikeouts and a 3.40 ERA. In total, he pitched 3,186 innings in the Majors and was an All-Star three times (1962 (2x), 1965).

Gimpy, however, is usually remembered for his role in two of the more memorable games in baseball: the so-called "asterisk" game in 1961, and

---

99 "Milt "Gimpy" Pappas and the Birth of a Nickname": http://baseballinteractions. wordpress.com/2011/03/31/milt-gimpy-pappas-and-the-birth-of-a-nickname/. Retrieved on August 8, 2014.

the almost perfect game he pitched in 1972. In 1961, Roger Maris was chasing Babe Ruth's single season home run record. On September 20th, Maris faced Pappas on the 154th game of the season. Commissioner Ford Frick had previously said that if Maris could not surpass Babe's mark by the 154th game, any homers after that would mean his final record would include an asterisk: after 1961, the season had been extended to 162 games, whereas Babe only had 154 games to hit 60 home runs in 1927. That Maris's achievement might forever be a "qualified" record did not sit well with Gimpy. According to Pappas, the night before the game, he approached Maris with some important information: "I told him that I was going to give him nothing but fastballs tomorrow. Maris said, "Really?!" I told him, "Absolutely."[100] Gimpy went on to say that Mantle, who was with Maris that evening, asked him if he would get all fastballs also? The answer was simply, "you're on your own big boy". Indeed, Maris hit his 59th homer that game. Gimpy mused that had he stayed in the game, Maris might have tied Babe's record that day. Maris did go on to beat Babe's record that year, getting his 61st home run on October 1st. The pitcher in that game was Tracey Stallard of the Red Sox.

The second notable game was on September 2nd, 1972. The place was Wrigley Field. The opposing team was the San Diego Padres. Pappas had retired the first 26 batters and needed just one more strike to make it a perfect game. According to Gimpy, "Larry Stahl was sent up to pinch-hit and I got two strikes on him immediately. Randy Hundley (the Cubs' catcher) called for a slider. Ball one. Slider. Ball two. Slider. Ball three. Slider. Ball four. Stahl walks and the perfect game is gone."[101] Pappas felt that he had been robbed, and that any of the four called balls were easily strikes. When the umpire, Bruce Froemming came out to the mound after Stahl reached first, Gimpy called him "every name that I knew in the English language. When I ran out of names in English, I started calling him names in Greek."[102] The next day Froemming asked Pappas to sign a baseball to commemorate his nearly perfect outing. Gimpy did, but then offered up

---

100 Bruce Amspacher, "What Really Happened? An Interview with Major League Pitching Great Milt Pappas." PSA Sports (April 11, 2003): http://www.psacard.com/Articles/ArticleView/3819/what-really-happened-an-interview-with-major-league-pitching-great-milt-pappas. Retrieved on August 8, 2014.

101 Ibid

102 Ibid

some unsolicited advice regarding where the ball might best be kept for safekeeping. Anatomically, it would have been difficult (and painful) for Froemming to heed the advice.

On September 24th, 1971, Gimpy pitched a perfect inning against the Phillies. In the top of the 4th, facing the 6th, 7th and 8th, Pappas retired Greg Luzinski, who struck out swinging, got Don Money looking at strike three, and Mike Anderson who like Luzinki, missed the third pitch swinging away.[103] Despite his performance in the 4th inning, Pappas would give up 5 runs that game, over 6.2 innings of work. The Phillies, who at that point in the year were 65-93, would go onto win, 6-1. Mike Anderson garnered 2 RBIs on 2 hits.

Five days after his immaculate inning, Pappas would again make baseball history. Pitching against the Montreal Expos, he hit Ron Hunt, making Hunt the first player to be hit 50 times by a pitch in a single season, which bettered by one, the previous record set by Hughie Jennings in 1896. Once again, Gimpy blamed the umpire for a bad call, claiming Hunt made no effort to avoid a pitch that was clearly over the plate. Hunt was pretty adept at making a hit look legitimate; he would later break his own record, making fifty-one the new benchmark.

At the time this chapter was written, Milt Pappas was 75 years old. Life after baseball was anything but kind to the ex-pitcher. In 1982, Carole Pappas, his wife of twenty-two years, disappeared. Nearly five years to the day she went missing, construction workers found her car and her body while draining a pond just a short distance from their home.[104] While it was suspected that the incident may have been caused by alcohol (Carole was a recovering alcoholic), neither this nor foul play was the official explanation. Another automobile related accident, this time to Pappas himself, would occur in February of 2013. He crashed his Jeep into a utility pole, which resulted in eight broken ribs and a laceration to his ear.[105]

---

103 "September 24, 1971 Philadelphia Phillies at Chicago Cubs Play by Play and Box Score," Baseball-Reference: http://www.baseball-reference.com/boxes/CHN/CHN197109240. shtml Retrieved August on 8, 2014.

104 Jack Houston and John O'Brien, "Pappas Identified No Sign Of Foul Play," *Chicago Tribune*, (August 09, 1987): http://articles.chicagotribune.com/1987-08-09/news/8702280450_1_ mrs-pappas-carole-pappas-milt-pappas. Retrieved August on August 8, 2014.

105 Phil Angelo, "After accident, Pappas on road to recovery," *The Daily Journal*: http://www. daily-journal.com/sports/after-accident-pappas-on-road-to-recovery/article_31261ea9-94d9-52c2-a587-3a587852b20d.html. Retrieved on August 8, 2014.

Bruce Sutter
September 8th, 1977

In September of 1977, in a year that saw the release of the first Star Wars movie, the release (firing) of the punk rock band the Sex Pistols from EMI records, and the incorporation of Apple Computers, another Hall of Fame pitcher recorded a perfect nine-pitch, three-out inning. Howard Bruce Sutter was born on January 8th, 1953 in Lancaster, Pennsylvania. Signed as an amateur free agent by the Cubs in '71, he made his first appearance in the Majors for the Cubbies on May 9th, 1976. He played for twelve seasons in the Majors, on three different clubs: Chicago Cubs (1976-1980), the St. Louis Cardinals (1981-1984) and the Atlanta Braves (1985-86, 1988).[106] A right-handed relief pitcher, Sutter relied mainly on a split-fingered fastball, fastball and slider to get the job done. In fact, Sutter is credited with popularizing the split-fingered fastball, which he learned from Fred Martin, the Cubs minor league instructor, in 1973.[107] Dick Williams remarked that Sutter's split-finger pitch was " unhittable, unless he hangs it, and he never does. It's worse than trying to hit a knuckleball."[108]

---

106 "Bruce Sutter Player Page," Baseball Reference: http://www.baseball-reference.com/players/s/suttebr01.shtml. Retrieved on November 7, 2014.

107 James and Neyer, Op Cit., pp.398.

108 "Bruce Sutter's Hall of Fame Page," Baseball Hall of Fame: http://baseballhall.org/hof/sutter-bruce. Retrieved on November 7, 2014.

Over his career, Sutter posted a 68-71 record, 2.83 ERA, 861 strike-outs and 300 saves over 661 games. He made six All-Star Teams (1977-81, 1984), played on the 1982 Cardinals team that won the World Series, and won the National League Cy Young award in '79. Additionally, Sutter was named the National League Rolaids Relief Man of the Year a total of four times (1979, 1981, 1982, 1984). He was inducted into the Hall of Fame in 2006, on the thirteenth ballot in his thirteenth year of eligibility (capturing 76.9% of the vote).

Sutter pitched his perfect inning on September 8th, 1977, in a game against the Expos at Wrigley Field. The starting pitcher for the Cubs that game was Ray Burris. Burris would pitch 6 innings before being relieved by Paul Reuschel in the top of the 7th. By that point, the Cubs were behind by 2 runs. In the bottom of the inning, Jerry Morales came into the game, pinch-hitting for Reuschel. The Cubs would tie the game before the inning was over. Sutter replaced Morales in the line-up, coming in to pitch in the top of the 8th. Facing Warren Cromartie, Andre Dawson and Tony Perez, Sutter would get a near-immaculate inning, striking out all three but with the second out requiring a throw from catcher George Mitterwald to first base to retire Dawson. The score would remain tied through to the top of the 9th, when Sutter again took the mound. This time facing Ellis Valentine, Gary Carter and Larry Parrish, Sutter struck out all three on just nine pitches. The game went into extra innings until a Bill Buckner sac fly in the 10th enabled the Cubs to win 3-2. Sutter would get the win, pitching 3 innings allowing only 1 hit, no runs, 1 walk, while recording 6 strikeouts.

Sutter underwent shoulder surgery in February, 1987, and missed the entire season.[109] When he returned in 1988, he was unable to match his previous performances, playing in thirty-eight games with a 4.76 ERA. That same year, he underwent surgery on his right knee and by 1989, owing to continued shoulder problems, he left baseball for good, playing his last game for the Braves on September 9th, 1988. On September 17th, 2006, Sutter's number 42 was retired by the Cards during an on-field ceremony. Whitey Herzog, Sutter's manager in the '82 World Series had this say to about his player: "In my 40-some years of professional baseball, he

---

109 "Atlanta Braves relief pitcher Bruce Sutter plans to..." *Chicago Tribune* (January 23, 1987): http://articles.chicagotribune.com/1987-01-23/sports/8701060551_1_contract-al-pitcher-outfielder-max-venable. Retrieved November on 8, 2014.

was by far the most dominant and best reliever I've ever seen."[110] Sutter's son Chad also played baseball, first for Tulane University and then one season in the minors for the Yankees. On August 23rd, 2010, Sutter became a minor league consultant for the Phillies, evaluating pitching prospects in that club's double- and triple-A affiliates. In November of that same year, he was inducted into the St. Louis Hall of Fame. Finally, in January of 2014, he was inducted into the St Louis Cardinals' Hall of Fame Museum. At the time this chapter was written, he was 61 years old.

110 "42 closed for Cards forever: Sutter's jersey retired," *Associated Press* reprinted in ESPN. com: http://sports.espn.go.com/mlb/news/story?id=2591746. Retrieved on November 7, 2014.

Pedro Borbón
June 23rd, 1979

One of the four pitchers to make the front cover of this book was also the twenty-first pitcher to record an immaculate inning. Pedro Borbón Rodriguez was born in the Dominican Republic on December 2nd, 1946. A right-handed reliever, the report on his pitch selection simply lists, "fastball". It does go on to describe however, it was a lively ball, quoting Sparky Anderson, who also described his fastball as having great movement.[111] Borbón played twelve seasons in the Majors for four different ball clubs: the Angels (1969), the Cincinnati Reds (1970-79), the San Francisco Giants (1979) and finally, the St. Louis Cardinals (1980). Originally drafted as a free agent by the Cardinals in '64, Borbón made his debut with the California Angels on April 9th, 1969. He posted a career record of 69-39, 3.52 ERA, 409 strikeouts and 80 saves. He was part of two great Cincinnati Reds World Series teams in 1975 and 1976.[112]

It is difficult not to notice that where Borbón is concerned, there is more than one on-field instance of biting that occurred during his career. Both, not surprisingly, also involved fighting. The first began as a case of mistaken hat identity. In 1973, after a bench-clearing brawl involving Borbón's Reds

---

111 James and Neyer, Op Cit, pp.138.
112 "Pedro Borbon Player Page," Baseball Reference: http://www.baseball-reference.com/players/b/borbope01.shtml. Retrieved October on 13, 2013.

and the New York Mets, Borbón, having just fought a couple of rounds with Mets catcher Buzz Capra, picked up what he thought was a Reds cap and put it on his head, only to realize he had grabbed a Mets cap instead. His reaction? He took a bite out of it.[113] A year later in 1974 he was involved in another fight, this time involving Pirates pitcher Daryl Patterson. Borbón pulled hair and took a bite out of the poor hurler, while he had him pinned to the turf. Patterson later had to have a tetanus shot, just to be on the safe side. The following day, the public address announcer in Pittsburgh introduced Borbón as Dracula.[114] If biting (and hair pulling) were not enough, Borbón has also been implicated in another strange incident, this time involving voodoo. Upset at being traded to the Giants, Borbón is said to have placed a curse on the Reds and their stadium.[115] Though sources are scarce, at least one writer claims that Hal McCoy of the *Dayton Daily News* confirmed the accuracy of story. According to the same writer, Borbón was a believer of voodoo and curses, and also was a fan of cockfighting.[116] In 2002 however, Borbón denied putting a curse on Riverfront. Not that he sloughed it off as complete non-sense however; merely that he lacked the power to actually do it. Add to this that Borbón was also a licensed barber, I think it is safe to say that alongside Rube Waddell, he is certainly one of the most colourful pitchers to make this collection.

Borbón's immaculate inning came on June 23rd, 1979, in the 9th inning of a game in which his Reds faced the San Francisco Giants. With his team already behind by 3 runs, Borbón entered the game replacing Junior Kennedy, who was pinch-hitting for Fred Norman. The first two hitters, Mike Sadek and Gary Lavelle, both struck out swinging. Billy North, batting first in the lineup, stood looking at strike three. The Reds could not rally to make up the difference, and ended-up losing the game, 5-2.

Even after his retirement from the Majors, Borbón continued to play ball both in the Dominican and on semi-pro teams in Texas. He also remained

113 John Erardi, "Pedro Borbon, former Reds great, dead at 65. Dominican reliever had 'rubber arm' for Big Red Machine." *Cincinnati Enquirer* (June 5, 2012) reprinted in: http://archive.cincinnati.com/article/20120604/COL19/306040078/Pedro-Borbon-former-Reds-great-dead-65. Retrieved on November 4, 2014.

114 Spike Vrusho. *Benchclearing: Baseball's Greatest Fights and Riots.* Globe Pequot, 2008 pp. 47.

115 Ibid. John Erardi.

116 Brian Baker, "The Pedro Borbon Vodoo Hex," Chin Music: http://www.chinmusic. net/borbon.html. Retrieved on November 4, 2014.

active with the Reds organization, including participating in legends camps and in annual festivals hosted by his former team. His son, Pedro Borbón Jr., also became a pitcher, playing from 1992-2003 for the Braves, Dodgers, Blue Jays, Astros and Cardinals respectively. Like his dad, he was also on a World Series winning team—the 1995 Atlanta Braves. Tragically, Borbón died of cancer on June 4th, 2012. He was just 65 years old.[117]

---

117 "Pedro Borbon dies of cancer at 65" *Associated Press* reprinted in ESPN.com: http:// espn.go.com/mlb/story/_/id/8009018/former-cincinnati-reds-reliever-pedro-borbon-succumbs-cancer-65. Retrieved on October 3, 2014.

Lynn Everett McGlothen
August 25th, 1979

Lynn Everett McGlothen was the twenty-second pitcher to record an immaculate inning. His story, however, is one of the more tragic in this collection. Born in Monroe, Louisiana on March 27th, 1950, McGlothen attended Grambling High School and Grambling State University in Louisiana, until he was drafted third overall in the '68 amateur draft by the Red Sox. A right-handed pitcher, he made his Major League debut with Boston on June 25th, 1972. In a career that lasted eleven seasons from 1972 to 1982, Lynn played for a total of six different ball clubs: the Red Sox (1972-73), the St. Louis Cardinals (1974-76), the Giants (1977-78), the Chicago Cubs (1978-81) and the White Sox (1981), before making his final appearance on September 19th, 1982, with the New York Yankees. During his time in the Majors, he had an 86-93 record, 3.98 ERA, and 939 strikeouts over 1,497.2 innings. In 1974, while playing with the Cardinals, he was selected as an All-Star. That same season, he finished with a 16-12 record and 2.69 ERA.

In addition to retiring the side on nine pitches, McGlothen is also one of a very small number of pitchers who recorded at least six strikeouts in each of his first three games in the Majors. In 1980, while pitching for the Chicago Cubs, he also achieved another rare feat. Although he allowed 9 earned runs in a single game against the San Francisco Giants, he managed to still record the win thanks to an explosive offense that gave him 15 runs to work with that day. Overall that game, he pitched 7 and $\frac{2}{3}^{rds}$ innings, allowing 14 hits in the game.

On August 25th, 1979, in a game against the San Francisco Giants, McGlothen took the mound in the bottom of the 3rd, facing the top of the order in Larry Herndon, Joe Strain and Jack Clark. It took him nine pitches to retire the side, Strain and Clark struck out swinging, while Herndon was caught looking. Lynn would record the loss that day, pitching 6.1 innings, allowing 4 runs on 8 hits at Candlestick that afternoon. His Cubs were outscored, 5-2.

Toward the end of this career, McGlothen suffered from shoulder and elbow problems, spending much of the 1978 Major League season on the disabled list. In 1984, while visiting a friend in Dubach, Louisiana, McGlothen was killed in a fire that consumed the mobile home he was staying in at the time.[118] His friend, Gloria Reed Smith, managed to save her two younger children but tragically died when she unsuccessfully attempted to save McGlothen from the flames. He was just 34 years old.

118 "Lynn McGlothen Dies in Fire," *Times-Union* (Aug. 15 1984) pp. 14 retrieved from: http://news.google.com/newspapers?id=CEJHAAAAIBAJ&sjid=0HoMAAAAIBAJ&pg=4870,3166121&dq=lynn+mcglothen+fire&hl=en. Retrieved on September 16, 2014.

Joey McLaughlin
September 11th, 1979

The final immaculate inning pitched in the 1970s was by Joey McLaughlin, a right-handed relief pitcher born in Tulsa, Oklahoma on July 11th, 1956. He was drafted in the second round of the '74 amateur draft by the Atlanta Braves; he made his Major League debut with the same club on June 11th, 1977. In total, McLaughlin played seven seasons from '77 to '84 (missing 1978 altogether) for three different ball clubs: the Braves (1977, 1979), the Toronto Blue Jays (1980-84) and the Texas Rangers (1984). He had a career 29-28 win-loss record, with a 3.85 ERA, and 268 strikeouts.[119]

On September 11th, 1979, McLaughlin became the twenty-third pitcher in baseball history to retire the side on nine pitches. His perfect inning came in a game his Braves were playing against the San Francisco Giants at Candlestick Park. In the bottom of the 7th, McLaughlin replaced Mike Lum to face the Giants lineup. In order, McLaughlin struck out Larry Herndon (batting 5th), Greg Johnston, and Johnnie LeMaster, all swinging. McLaughlin finished the game and recorded a save, allowing only 2 hits, no runs, 4 strikeouts and a walk over 3 innings of play. The Braves won the game, 2-1.

After two seasons with the Braves, McLaughlin was traded to the Toronto Blue Jays along with teammates Barry Bonnell and Pat Rockett.

---

119 "Joey McLaughlin. Player Page," Baseball Reference: http://www.baseball-reference. com/players/m/mclaujo01.shtml?redir. Retrieved on November 7, 2014.

In 1982, Bobby Cox became the manager of the Jays, and while in '82 and '83, the club would finish sixth and fourth in the American League East, great things were coming later that decade. Alas, McLaughlin would not be a part of it. In 1983, his blown saves count outnumbered his saves, 11-9. Early in the '83 season, he was released by the Jays and eventually signed with the Texas Rangers. In his final year with Texas, he played in just fifteen games, finishing only five, with an ERA of 4.41. His last game in the Majors was on September 25th, 1984, and the Rangers released him at the end of the season.

As noted a few sections back, the 1970s were described as the era of the player, in recognition of the significant gains players made in relation to free agency and arbitration. By the 1980s, the movement of free agents between teams would help usher in the next era of baseball—the demise of team dynasties … at least for a period of time anyway.[120]

_____

120 Rader, Op Cit. pp. 221.

Ron Guidry
August 7th, 1984

In 1984, Van Halen released their sixth studio album, and their last with front man David Lee Roth for more than two decades (in 2012, the band reunited to record again). Simply titled *1984*, it came out in a year when many popular culture figures were capitalizing on the date to reflect on how much of Orwell's imagined hyper-surveillant society from his novel *1984* had indeed come to fruition. It was also the year that a film adaptation of the 1952 novel, *The Natural*, starring Robert Redford and Glenn Close, hit the big screen. Perhaps the success of that movie was its juxtaposition to Orwellian dystopia, as it depicted a simpler time that was more a part of baseball's mythology than its reality.

1984 was also the year that Ron Guidry pitched a perfect inning for the Yankees. The "Louisiana Lightning" or simply the "Gator", were the nicknames belonging to Ronald Ames Guidry, who was born on August 28th, 1950. A left-handed pitcher, he played fourteen years (1975-1988) in the Majors, all of them with the New York Yankees. He was Captain of that team from 1986 to 1988, a four-time All-Star (1978, 1979, 1982, 1983), part of two World Series Champion teams (1977, 1978), an American League Cy Young winner (1978), and winner of the Roberto Clemente Award in 1984.

Making his debut for the Yankees on July 27th, 1975, Guidry would complete his career with a 170-91 win-loss record, and a career ERA of

3.29 with 1778 strikeouts to his credit. In a career full of notable achievements, one of Guidry's most notable came in a one-game playoff to decide the 1978 American League East Division Championship against the Yanks' rival Boston Red Sox at Fenway. Guidry recorded his 25th win of the season that day, in a 3-2 victory over the Sox. The hero though was Bucky Dent, who hit a three-run homer off Mike Torrez to put his team ahead. Guidry actually gave up a home run to Carl Yastrzemski earlier in the game in the 2nd inning. The Yankees of course would go on to win the World Series in six games against the Dodgers. For Guidry, 1978 was a career year, ranked among the best in the modern era.

On August 7th, 1984, Guidry took the mound at the top of the 9th inning in a game against the Chicago White Sox. Facing the heart of the Sox line-up with Carlton Fisk, Tom Paciorek and Greg Luzinski, Guidry finished the game on successive strikeouts. The Yankees blanked the Sox 7-0. Having pitched a complete game shutout, Guidry allowed just 4 hits, issued no walks, and struck out 13 batters that afternoon.

Guidry's number 49 was retired by the Yankees on August 23rd, 2003. Teammate Reggie Jackson brought out the framed 49 commemorating the event. Guidry told the audience on hand that day at Yankee Stadium that one regret he had was not saying goodbye, and that he'd always tried to give them his best.[121] The plaque celebrating Guidry's achievement simply read: "A dominating pitcher and a respected leader. A true Yankee."

In 2006, Guidry returned to baseball and the Yankees, replacing Mel Stottlemyre as pitching coach under Joe Torre. It was not a good year for the Yankees pitching core however, and Guidry faced a lot of heat for their underperformance. When Torre left in 2007, Guidry's term as coach ended also. Guidry was 63 years old when this entry was completed.

---

121 "Guidry humbled by honor" Tom Singer. MLB.com: http://newyork.yankees.mlb.com/news/article.jsp?ymd=20030823&content_id=495068&vkey=news_nyy&fext=.jsp&c_id=nyy. Retrieved on August 8, 2014.

Danny Jackson
October 24th, 1985

Danny Lynn Jackson spent fifteen years in the Majors, from 1983 to 1997. His debut came on September 11th, 1983, for the Kansas City Royals. He would play for the Royals for five seasons (1983-1987) before moving to the Cincinnati Reds from 1988 to 1990. Over the next seven seasons, he would play for the Cubs (1991-92), Pirates (1992), Phillies (1993-94), Cardinals (1995-97) and finally for the Padres, making his last appearance in the Majors on August 7th, 1997. Overall, the lefty's career ended with a 112-131 record, 4.01 ERA, and 1,225 strikeouts. Jackson was twice named to the National League All-Star Team (1988, 1994), played on two World Series Champion teams (Royals in '85; Reds in '90); and was also part of the '93 Phillies that made it to the World Series. In 1988, he led the National League in wins with twenty-three.

Blue Jays fans will remember Jackson, but not with fondness. In the 1985 American League Championship Series, the Royals faced certain elimination, down 3-1. Starting in Game Five, Jackson threw a complete game, shutting out the Jays and keeping the Royals' hopes alive (Jackson faced Jimmy Key, who only allowed 2 runs on 8 hits). Stirred on by the impressive pitching performance of Jackson, the Royals rallied back, beating the Jays and moving on to the World Series. With the Series dubbed the I-70 Showdown because of the highway connecting both cities, Jackson was thrust back in the spotlight when he started Game Five. Once more, the Royals faced elimination, down three games to one against the St. Louis Cardinals. Jackson lead his club to victory one more time, and the Royals bounced back to take the Series and win the ultimate prize in professional baseball. To this day, his 1.04 post-season ERA stands as the lowest in Royals' history among pitchers with at least 10 innings played in post-season play.

On October 24th, 1985, Jackson started for the Royals at Busch Stadium II in St. Louis. He pitched all 9 innings, allowing just 1 run off 5 hits. In the bottom of the 7th, he faced the bottom of the order, with his team up by 3 runs. First up, Terry Pendleton went down swinging on strike three. Next came Tom Nieto, who was caught looking. Brian Harper, the third batter, came in as a pinch hitter for pitcher Todd Worrell, and struck out swinging on the 9th pitch of the inning. The Royals beat the Cardinals, 6-1. Significantly, this is the only immaculate inning to have occurred during in a World Series game.

Jackson was born in San Antonio, Texas on January 5th, 1962, making him 52 years old when this book was completed. After he departed professional baseball, he opened a family entertainment centre in Overland Park, Kansas, which includes a 40-lane bowling alley, arcade and an18-hole miniature golf course.[122]

---

122 "Where have you gone, Danny Jackson?" MLB.com: http://kansascity.royals.mlb. com/news/article.jsp?ymd=20020608&content_id=47050&vkey=news_kc&fext=. jsp&c_id=kc. Retrieved on April 28, 2014.

Jeff Robinson
September 7th, 1987

It would be two more years before another player pitched another perfect nine-pitch, strikeout inning. Jeffrey Daniel Robinson, a right-handed reliever, was not only the pitcher of record to break the drought, but was also the only pitcher to do so during the '87 season. Born on December 13th, 1960, the Santa Ana California native was actually first drafted in the fourteenth round of the '82 amateur draft by the Detroit Tigers, but declined to sign. The following year, he was drafted again by the San Francisco Giants in the second round. He began his career as a starter, making his debut for the Giants on April 7th, 1984. By 1986 however, following a rough season that lasted only eight games, he was sent to the bullpen as a reliever. In a career that spanned nine seasons, he finished with a 46-57 record, 3.79 ERA, and 629 strikeouts. During that time, he played for five different clubs: the Giants (1984-87), Pirates (1987-1989), Yankees (1990), Angels (1991) and Chicago Cubs (1992). He had three pitches in his arsenal: a split-fingered fastball, fastball and big curve.[123]

Although 1988 statistically speaking was Robinson's best year (11-5 record with a 3.03 ERA), 1987 was equally notable given two special events that occurred for him within a span of less than 72 hours. On September 7th, in a game against the Cubs at Wrigley Field, Robinson came into the

---

123 James and Neyer, Op Cit, pp. 361.

bottom of the 8th in relief of Brian Fisher. With his team ahead by 1 run, he faced the heart of the Cubs order in Leon Durham, Andre Dawson, and Rafael Palmeiro. All three batters struck out on a total of nine pitches. Robinson returned in the 9th, only giving up a single to Jerry Mumphrey, and the Pirates went on to win the game 3-2.

Two days later, in game three of the same series against the Cubs, Robinson achieved another first in his career. In the top of the 9th, batting in the number nine spot with two outs, Robinson hit a home run off Lee Smith to break a 3-3 tie. With the Cubs failing to score in the 9th, the Pirates went on to win the game 4-3 and swept the series. It was Robinson's second homer that season, one of only three he would hit in his career in the Majors.

Rob Dibble
June 4ᵗʰ, 1989

Robert Keith Dibble recorded the last immaculate inning pitched in the 1980s. Born on January 24ᵗʰ, 1964, the right-handed pitcher, a graduate of Southington High School in the Connecticut town of the same name, Dibble's first appeared in the Majors on June 29ᵗʰ, 1988, with the Cincinnati Reds, the same club he would pitch his immaculate inning with in '89. In total, Dibble spent seven seasons in the Majors with three clubs: the Reds, Chicago White Sox and finally the Brewers (his final game was on September 30ᵗʰ, 1995). He finished his career with a 27-25 record, 2.98 ERA, 645 strikeouts, and 89 saves. The highlight of his career came as a member of the Reds team that won the World Series in 1990, a year he also won the National League Championship Series MVP. In '90 and '91, he was also named to the National League All-Star team. Dibble also holds the distinction for being the fastest pitcher to record 500 career strikeouts; a milestone he reached in just 368 innings. In 1994, Dibble required surgery on his pitching arm, forcing him to miss the whole season due to injury. That he only pitched two more seasons afterwards can no doubt be attributed to that injury.

Dibble may be best remembered, however, for his temper, which led to a number of infamous brawls. In 1989, he started a bench-clearing brawl after hitting Mets' second baseman Tim Teufel in the back. Two years later, another incident saw Dibble caught attempting to hit Cub's outfielder Doug Dascenzo in the back as he ran down the first baseline. Earlier that same season, he was involved in a fight with Eric Yelding, a shortstop for the Astros. Dibble did not discriminate against fighting partners. In addition to players, he also went a round wrestling his manager Lou Piniella. The origin of the fight seems to be linked to Dibble having not been called in to close the game, and a discrepancy in the reasons why he remained in the bullpen that night. After having told reporters there was nothing wrong with his arm, unfortunately in contradiction to what Piniella had just told them, the two scuffled in the clubhouse, forcing teammates to intervene. The event would not go unnoticed as several reporters were present. All Piniella would say was "you saw it, write about it".[124] Given that the Reds had won, one wonders what exactly would have happened had they lost that evening in September to the Braves? Finally, again in 1991, Dibble was suspended for four games (and fined an undisclosed amount) for throwing a ball into the centre field stands, striking a poor fan, Meg Porter, in the elbow. Her injury required medical treatment, and cost the schoolteacher several days off.[125] Apparently, he was frustrated at having given up two runs before finally getting the last out of the game against the Cubs, in a game the Reds won 4-3 (again begging the question what would he have done had he blown the save?).

If Dibble was angry on the afternoon of June 4th, 1989, he did not show it. The Reds faced the San Diego Padres at Riverfront Stadium. Dibble got the call and came in relief of Danny Jackson in the 7th to get the last 2 outs of the inning. At the top of the 8th, he returned, protecting a 2-run lead against Padres hitters Martinez, Parent and Templeton. Parent was caught looking while the other two went down swinging. The Reds took the game, 5-3.

Controversy continues to follow Dibble, who spent the last two decades as a sport commentator for a number of national and regional broadcasters. Among the more recent instances, he was soundly criticized for telling Washington National's Rookie pitcher Strasburg to "suck it up" in relation to his serious arm injury.[126] He was 50 years old when this book was written.

---

124 "Piniella, Dibble Brawl in Clubhouse," *Los Angeles Times*, (September 18, 1992), np.

125 "A New Suspension for Reds' Dibble," *New York Times*, (May 4, 1991), np.

126 "Stephen Strasburg needs second MRI," ESPN.com: http://sports.espn.go.com/mlb/news/story?id=5497876 Retrieved on August 1, 2014.

JOHN CLARKSON.
ALLEN & GINTER'S
RICHMOND. Cigarettes VIRGINIA.

WADDELL, ST. LOUIS AMER.

Hall of Famer John Clarkson was the first pitcher in the history of the game to pitch an immaculate inning.

The second pitcher in MLB history to pitch an immaculate ainning, Rube Waddell tragically died young from complications following an attempt to save a local town from rising flood waters.

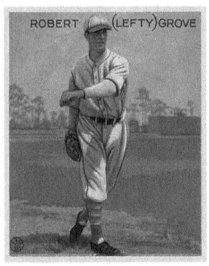

ROBERT (LEFTY) GROVE

Hall of Famer Lefty Grove was a fierce competitor during the 1920s and was the first to record more than one immaculate inning.

RAGAN-BROOKLYN-NAT.

Pat Ragan was known for his showmanship and flair. Ragan was the third pitcher in MLB history to record an immaculate inning; arguably the only notable achievement in his career.

Dazzy Vance, known for his devastating fastball and a ripped shirt that served to distract batters, was the sixth pitcher in MLB history to record an immaculate inning

Tony Cloninger broke up Sandy Koufax's streak of consecutive immaculate innings with his own perfect inning in 1963.

Dominant left-hander Sandy Koufax holds the distinction of being the only MLB pitcher to record three immaculate innings.

Pedro Borbón was a figure of considerable controversy due to his unusual behavior. He recorded the first of four immaculate innings in 1979 while with the Cincinnati Reds.

Hall of Fame pitcher Nolan Ryan tossed two immaculate innings for two different teams in both leagues during his long and impressive career.

The "Big Unit" Randy Johnson, now in the Hall of Fame, is one of the select few to pitch more than one immaculate inning.

PART IV: 1990-2000

Jeff Montgomery
April 29th, 1990

Jeff Montgomery's perfect inning was the first and only of the '90 season and the first of the decade. Born in Wellston, Ohio on January 7th, 1962, Montgomery was a righted-handed relief pitcher who played thirteen seasons in the Majors, mostly for the Kansas City Royals. Drafted by the Cincinnati Reds in the ninth round of the '83 amateur draft, he made his big league debut on August 1st, 1987, for that club. He was traded to the Kansas City Royals in 1988 for Van Snider, an outfielder and pinch hitter. There he would finish his career, and have his greatest success as a reliever. Montgomery pitched 700 innings, recording 46 wins and 52 losses. He had a career 3.27 ERA, with 733 strikeouts, and 304 saves. In the twelve seasons he played with the Royals (1988-1999), he was named to the American League All-Star Team three times, in 1992, 1993 and 1996. In 1993, he also won the American League Rolaids Relief Man of the Year, a year in which he posted 45 saves for the Royals. He played his final game on October 2nd, 1999, for KC.

One of the distinguishing things about Montgomery was his command over not one, but four different pitches. While most closers typically rely on one or maybe two pitches (typically a fastball with or without a curve or slider), Jeff could unleash fastballs, sliders, curves and change-ups on hitters and did so regularly.[128] To Montgomery though, when asked what

---

128 James and Neyer, Op Cit, p. 313.

his best pitch was, he simply said a strike. He went on to say, "if I had to narrow it down, I got more quality outs over my career on a slider."[129]

On April 29th, 1990, Montgomery added pitching an immaculate inning to his career statistics. Facing the Texas Rangers at Royals Stadium for a Sunday afternoon game, Montgomery replaced Larry McWilliams on the mound in the top of the 8th. He quickly dismissed Pete Incaviglia, Geno Petralli and Thad Bosley, each of whom were retired on three pitches. Montgomery recorded the win, working from a 3-run lead. He played a total of 2 innings, allowing no hits or walks while chalking up an impressive 13 strikeouts on the day. The Royals beat the Rangers, 5-2.

While he did not make it to Cooperstown, collecting only .4% of the vote in 2005, he is forever enshrined in the Royals' Hall of Fame where his career number of saves places him easily in the discussion as perhaps the Royals' best reliever. His former Manager, Herk Robinson, had this to say about his reliever, reflecting on his career before his installment in the Hall: "He was always there when you needed him. He was probably one of those guys you always took for granted a little bit. He had good stuff, though. He was a four-pitch pitcher who could usually get two or three pitches over in any game. When you can do that, you're going to be tough. He wasn't an intimidator, but he was a heck of a pitcher."[130]

Life after baseball has been busy for Montgomery. In addition to making an instructional video on pitching, entitled *Fundamentals of Pitching with Jeff Montgomery*, he served as Vice-President of Union Broadcasting in Kansas City Missouri. In 2010, he was hired by Fox Sports Kansas City, as a part-time colour commentator for the Royals, and analyst for the pre-game Royals Live show.

---

129 Bob Dutton, "Royals to save a space for Montgomery in Hall," *The Kansas City Star*, (December 5, 2002), D1.

130 Dutton, Ibid.

Andy Ashby
June 15th, 1991

The first of the '91 triumvirate of pitchers to record a perfect inning was Andrew Jason Ashby. The right-handed starting pitcher was born in Kansas City, Missouri on July 11th, 1967. He was signed as an undrafted free agent by the Phillies in 1986 and made his debut in the Majors for that club on June 10th, 1991. His career spanned fourteen seasons, pitching for the Phillies (1991-92, 2000), Colorado Rockies (1993), San Diego Padres (1993-99, 2004), Atlanta Braves (2000), and the Los Angeles Dodgers (2001-03). His final appearance in the Majors came as a Padre on September 14th, 2004. Over his career, Ashby had a 98-110 record, 4.12 ERA, and 1,173 strikeouts over 1810.2 innings pitched.

His best years were with San Diego where he was named an All-Star in back-to-back seasons (1998 and 1999). In 1998, he was a key part of that Padres team that made it to the World Series, with a 17-9 record and a 3.34 ERA. Unfortunately for San Diego fans, their team faced the powerhouse Yankees in the fall classic. Under Joe Torre, the Yanks had a line-up that included Derek Jeter, Jorge Posada, Tim Raines and Darryl Strawberry and a pitching staff with the likes of David Wells, David Cone and Orlando Hernández that was simply too much for the Padres. The Yankees swept the Series in four games. Ashby was the starter for Game Two, giving up 7 runs in the first 2 innings.

On June 15th, 1991, Ashby became the twenty-ninth in MLB history to record an immaculate inning. Already down by 3 runs to start the 4th,

Ashby faced Hal Morris, Todd Benzinger and Jeff Reed, striking out the side in order on nine pitches. The Phillies however, would not be able to catch the Reds, and lost 3-1. Ashby was tagged with the loss, pitching a total of 5 innings, giving up 4 hits and 3 earned runs. After the game, Ashby said: "The record is pretty neat. I didn't realize I had made history until a reporter told me about it after the game. I'd never even done that in Little League. I only wish I had been that aggressive right from the start."[131] In terms of his approach, he remarked: "I wanted my curve in the dirt and that's where I put it. I guess they looked good because they swung at them. On Reed, it was supposed to be a fastball outside but it wound up right down the middle. I caught a break when he missed it."[132]

Ashby suffered several injuries to his shoulder, elbow and back throughout his career that made it tough to continue pitching. In 2003, he had Tommy John surgery and never really recovered. He was finally released in 2006, during Spring Training, and officially retired from the game.

---

131 Don Bostrom, "Ashby Gets Record But Reds Get Win," *The Morning Call* (June 16, 1991): http://articles.mcall.com/1991-06-16/sports/2794072_1_rare-feat-andy-ashby-hurler. Retrieved on October 3, 2014.

132 Ibid

David Cone
August 30th, 1991

After Ashby, David Cone was the second pitcher to record an immaculate inning in that '91 season. Born on January 2nd, 1963, in Kansas City, Missouri, David Brian Cone played seventeen seasons in the majors before playing his last game, for the New York Mets, on May 28th, 2003, at the age of 40. Drafted by the Royals in the third round of the amateur draft in 1981, he made his debut on June 8th, 1986. Cone would play for six different teams over his long and impressive career: Kansas City Royals (1986, 1993-94), New York Mets (1987-1992, 2003), Toronto Blue Jays (1992, 1995), New York Yankees (1995-2000) and the Boston Red Sox (2001). While in the era of free agency, it is no longer surprising for a player to play for many different, even rival, clubs; what makes Cone's journey somewhat more notable is the number of clubs he played with multiple times. For example, be played for the Jays twice, first in 1992, then again in 1995. He did the same with both the Royals and the Mets.[133]

A right-handed starting pitcher, Cone began his career with four pitches in his arsenal: a fastball (mid-90s), slider, sharp curve and change-up. Later on, as the velocity on his fastball began to dip, he added a splitter, overhand curve and sidearm (or Laredo) curve to the list. Cone had that special

---

133 "David Cone Player Page," Baseball Reference: http://www.baseball-reference.com/players/c/coneda01.shtml. Retrieved on December 2, 2014.

ability to change his arm-angle when throwing a fastball, which served to baffle even the best of hitters. His control, particularly his ability to paint the corners, was also highly respected.[134]

Cone retired with a career record of 194 wins, 126 losses, an ERA of 3.46, and 2,688 strikeouts. He won the Cy Young in 1994 (also voted in the top five for the award fives times), was a World Series Champion five times (1992, 1996, 1998-2000), a five-time All-Star (1988, 1992, 1994, 1997, 1999), three-time National League strikeout champion (1990-92), and the American League wins champion in 1998. In addition to a perfect inning, he also pitched a perfect game. He holds the distinction of being the only pitcher in major league history to win 20 games for both the Yankees and the Mets.[135]

On August 30th, 1991, at Riverfront Stadium in Cincinnati, Cone became the thirtieth pitcher in Major League history to pitch an immaculate inning. The Mets were facing the Reds that day and Cone was the starter. In the bottom of the 5th, Cone took the mound to face the bottom (8 and 9) and top of the order in the Reds lineup in Herm Winningham, Randy Myers, and Mariano Duncan. The game was tied 1-1 at that point, and would remain so as Cone shut down the side on nine pitches. All three batters struck out swinging. Cone would return for one more inning in the 6th, before leaving the game having allowed a run off a Paul O'Neill double (Kevin Elster was called in to pinch hit for the starter in the 7th). Cone would ultimately get the win, playing 6 innings, allowing 2 earned runs on 6 hits, striking out 9 batters and issuing only 1 walk. The final score was 3 to 2.

As a Blue Jays fan, I cannot help but comment on the role David Cone played in that club's first World Series Championship. I remember very well the trade that sent highly touted prospects Jeff Kent and Ryan Thompson to the Mets for Cone on August 27th, 1992. Although Kent went on to have a fine career, it is not like the Jays suffered with the acquisition of Alomar at second base (Kent's position). At that point in the season, the Jays had to do something, as they had failed to put significant ground between them and the Orioles and Brewers. Pat Gillick, then general manager for the Jays, was no stranger to late season trades for "rental" pitching. Bud Black from Cleveland in 1989, John Candelaria from the Twins in 1990, and Tom

---

134 James and Neyer, Op Cit, p.169-70.

135 Baseball Reference, Op Cit.

Candiotti also from the Indians in '91 were all late season pitching acquisitions, none of whom re-signed with the club the following season. As for Cone, for the reminder of that 1992 season, he would help the Jays secure the American League East, going 4 and 3 with a 2.55 ERA and 47 strikeouts. The Jays would go on to beat the Oakland As to take the American League Championship, and then defeat the Atlanta Braves in six games. Cone was the starter for Game Two in the World Series but was pulled by manager Cito Gaston after giving up 4 runs to Atlanta. It would be Duane Ward, not David Cone, who would get the win that day. Overall, Cone went 1-1 with a 3.22 ERA in the Jays postseason campaign that year.

Some readers may recall the link between Cone and the popular late night comedy show, Saturday Night Live. Fans of the pitcher are called "Cone-heads", inspired by the skit of the same name featuring Dan Aykroyd and Jane Curtin as pointy-headed aliens from the planet Remulak. The popularity of rubber Cone-heads is alive and well to this day at the home of the Buffalo Bisons' Coca-Cola Field. One of the beer vendors comes to each home game dawning a rubber cone-head, and proclaiming the cone-head guarantee, "if you get a warm beer from me, you drink it for free." At least from the vantage point of my seat, he has never had to pay-up yet.

Pete Harnisch
September 6th, 1991

Peter Thomas Harnisch was a righted-handed starting pitcher who played fourteen seasons in the Majors. Over his career, he played for the Orioles (1988-90), Astros (1991-94), Mets (1995-97), Brewers (1997), Reds (1998-2001) and Colorado Rockies (2002). His careers stats include a 111-103 record, 3.89 ERA, and 1,368 strikeouts. He was also the thirty-first pitcher in the Majors to pitch a perfect inning.

Born in Commack, New York, on September 23rd, 1966, Harnisch played NCAA baseball for Fordham University, where he majored in accounting. A first round pick in the 1987 MLB draft, he was the twenty-seventh player selected that round, by the Orioles. While at Fordham, he posted an impressive 21-3 record, 2.29 ERA and 213 strikeouts over 204 innings.[136] In 1990, Harnisch, Curt Schilling, and Steve Finley were traded to the Houston Astros for All-Star ('86 and '89) and Silver Slugger ('86) Glenn Davis. One of the worst trades in history, Davis would turn out to be a disappointment for the Orioles, and was released in 1993 after a string of injuries and disappointing performances. While with the Astros, Harnisch recorded many notable achievements. In addition to his

---

136 "Fordham Star Signs," *New York Times*, (June 9th, 1987): http://www.nytimes.com/1987/06/09/sports/sports-people-fordham-star-signs.html?src=pm. Retrieved on September 28, 2014.

immaculate inning, he made the All-Star Team in 1991. His best season statistically came in 1993, when he went 16-9 with a 2.98 ERA and 185 strikeouts. He would also tie Jack McDowell of the White Sox that year for most shutouts in a single season (4 in total).

However, following that successful season in '93, health issues ultimately lead to his demise in the Majors. Beginning with a tendon injury to his pitching arm in 1994, Harnisch was eventually traded to the New York Mets in 1995 where he was anything but impressive. Mets fan will remember that both Harnisch and Bret Saberhagen were the much-celebrated aces that would surely win them at least the Division. Instead, the duo went 7-13. As if their performance was not disappointing enough, on May 11, 1996, Harnisch was suspended for eight games for starting an on-field brawl when he threw an open-hand punch to the face of Chicago Cubs catcher Scott Servais.[137]

In 1997, Harnisch went public to tell a group of sportswriters during a teleconference that he had been diagnosed with major depression. He described his condition as a "chemical imbalance," which was possibly brought on when he quit using chewing tobacco just before the end of spring training.[138] Although smokeless tobacco is known to be associated with cancer, particular of the mouth, tongue and throat, the role it plays in the onset of depression is far from clear. In relation to cause, it seems far more likely that Harnisch's depression could be attributed to both the stress of playing the game, and/or a family history of the disorder. After four months on the disabled list, Harnisch returned to regular play, but was moved to the bullpen after three starts where his ERA skyrocketed to over 8. Later that same season, he was moved to the Milwaukee Brewers.

On September 6th, 1991, Harnisch was starting pitcher for the Astros, playing at home against the Phillies. In the top of the 7th, Harnisch faced the bottom of the order, with the game tied 1-1. First up, Wes Chamberlain, was retired on three pitches, swinging on the last offering. Dickie Thon went down looking at strike three while, José de Jesús was retired swinging

---

137 "BASEBALL: Harnisch Faces A Suspension,". *New York Times*, (May 14, 1996): http://www.nytimes.com/1996/05/14/sports/baseball-harnisch-faces-a-suspension. html?ref=peteharnisch. Retrieved on September 26, 2014.

138 Buster Olney, "Harnisch Says He Is Being Treated for Depression,". *New York Times*, (April 26, 1997): http://www.nytimes.com/1997/04/26/sports/harnisch-says-he-is-being-treated-for-depression.html. Retrieved on September 26, 2014.

on the 9th pitch of the inning. In the bottom of that same inning, Cedeno would hit a solo home run to put the Astros ahead. Al Osuna would come into the game in relief of Harnisch to the start the bottom of the 8th. He prevented any further runs for the reminder of the game and the Astros would go on to win, 3-1. Recording the win, Harnisch pitched 7 innings allowing only 1 run on 4 hits, while striking out a total of 12 batters.

In 1998, Harnisch would once again record numbers reminiscent of his best years with Houston. Although the Astros would finish fourth in the National League Central that season, Harnisch finished with a 14-7 record and a 3.14 ERA. The following season, he notched a 16-10 record for a much improved Reds team that tied the Mets for the Wild Card spot in the National League. The Reds unfortunately lost to the Mets in the play-in game. In 2003, Harnisch unsuccessfully attempted a comeback with the Reds Triple A Affiliate club, the Louisville Bats. After that, he would never again play professional baseball.

Trevor Wilson
June 7th, 1992

The only immaculate inning to occur in the 1992 season came from Trevor Wilson, a left-handed pitcher who played eight seasons in the Majors. Born on June 7th, 1966, in Torrance California, Trevor Kirk Wilson was drafted by the San Francisco Giants in the eighth round of the '85 amateur draft. He made his debut with the Giants on September 5th, 1988, a club he would remain part of from 1988 to 1993, before again returning in 1995. Shoulder surgery caused him to miss the 1994 season altogether (he also missed '96 and '97 owing to injuries). After signing as a free agent with the Cincinnati Reds in January, 1996, Wilson was released in April. He played his final season with the Anaheim Angels in 1998. Wilson finished with a 41-46 record, 3.87 ERA and 431 strikeouts.

On June 7th, 1992, Wilson started at Candlestick against a struggling Houston Astros team (25-30). In the top of the 9th, he faced the middle of the order in Jeff Bagwell, Eric Anthony and Rafael Ramírez. Pitching with a 3-run lead, all three batters stuck out swinging on nine pitches. Wilson pitched a complete game for the win, allowing just 2 hits and striking out 6 batters. It should also be noted that Wilson accomplished this feat on his birthday—the first of only two pitchers to do so.

Beyond his perfect inning, Wilson is also remembered for his near-miss no-hitter. In fact, it was a near perfect game. On just his second start on June 13th, 1990, Wilson had made it to the 9th with a no-hitter, when Mike

Pagliarulo from the Padres hit one to left-centre for a base hit, ending the streak. According to Wilson, "I didn't really expect to throw a no-hitter, so when it didn't happen, it's not like a big panic. I really wanted to get it, but I guess I'll have to settle for a one-hitter."[139] But for Pagliarulo's hit and for a wild pitch in the 5th on strike three, Wilson would have joined an even more rarified fraternity of perfect game pitchers.

His last game was with the Angels on September 26th, 1998. The 48-year old ex-pitcher remained in the game however, serving as a pitching coach in the minor leagues for the Arkansas Travelers, the Double-A affiliate for the Angels.

---

139 "Wilson One Hits the Padres," Associated Press in *Rome New Tribune*, (June 14 1990), 3B as reprinted in: http://news.google.com/newspapers?id=Al0jAAAAIBAJ &sjid=JDYDAAAAIBAJ&dq=trevor-wilson&pg=1094%2C3471443. Retrieved on October 5, 2014.

Mel Rojas
May 11ᵗʰ, 1994

Melquiades Rojas Medrano was born on December 10ᵗʰ, 1966, in Bajos de Haina in the Dominican Republic. Nicknamed "the Arsonist", Rojas played for ten years in the Majors for five different clubs: the Montreal Expos (1990-1996), Chicago Cubs (1997), New York Mets (1997-98), Los Angeles Dodgers (1999), Detroit Tigers (1999) and again for the Expos (1999) during his final season. According to the scouting report, Rojas used three pitches: a fastball, forkball and slider.[140] Signed by the Expos as an amateur free agent in '85, he made his debut in the Majors at the age of 23, playing for the Expos on August 1ˢᵗ, 1990. Over his career, he recorded a 34-31 record, 3.82 ERA, 562 strikeouts and 126 saves. His best year was 1992, where he had a win-loss percentage of .875 (7-1) and a 1.43 ERA, as a reliever with Montreal. In just over 100 innings pitched that season, he allowed only 16 earned runs and recorded 70 strikeouts.

However, his most notable achievement was pitching a perfect inning. On May 11ᵗʰ, 1994, the Expos played the Mets at home. In the top of the 9ᵗʰ, facing the bottom of the order, Rojas took the mound to protect a slim 1-run lead. Both David Segui and Todd Hundley struck out swinging. Jeff McKnight then came into the ballgame to pinch hit for Roger Mason (the pitcher) and, like his teammates went down swinging on strike three. Over

---

140 James and Neyer, Op Cit, p.363.

two innings pitched, Rojas allowed just 1 hit and 1 walk, picking up the save and ensuring a win for Pedro Martínez.

Although still early in the season, the Expos were 17-15 on May 11th when Rojas pitched a perfect 9th. Expo fans will of course remember 1994 as the season of dashed hopes and dreams. The team finished the season with a 74-40 record, the best in Major League Baseball. The Expos had not made to the post-season since 1981. But we will never know how the season would have finished or if the Expos would have gone to the World Series, as the season was cancelled on August 12th due to the ongoing players' strike. The World Series was cancelled that year, only the second time (1904 being the other) in the history of the game. As both a Canadian and a baseball fan, it is difficult not to be more than a little upset at what happened to the Montreal Expos. In 1994, the Expos were arguably the best team in baseball. The lock-out and strike that ultimately cancelled both the season and the Word Series, and darn near ruined the game permanently, not only ensured the Expos would not have a shot at being champions, but was the start of what would ultimately be a slow, ten-year demise for that team: by 2004, there was no major league team in *La Belle* Province. Some twenty years later, in March of 2014, over 96,000 fans attended two preseason games at the old Olympic Stadium in Montreal. Although Canada's team is the Blue Jays (simply because there is no other option in the MLB any way), and the Jays were the home team on the field that day, the number of fans who came to the park wearing Expos hats and shirts that day easily made it feel like old times at the Big 'O'. Indeed, I am no longer surprised to see Expos hats in the stands at the Rogers Centre (current home of the Blue Jays), or even in the playground at my children's primary school. There is still palpable hope in the air around here that Major League Baseball may indeed one day come to Montreal again.

Before finishing, as there is considerable interest in the genetics of sports performance and ability these days, I would be remiss if I did not acknowledge the familial transmission of the baseball gene in the Rojas' family tree. [141] He is the nephew of Felipe, Jesús and Matty Alou, and cousin of Moisés Alou, all of whom had impressive Major League careers. His son, Mel Rojas Jr. was drafted by the Pirates in 2010 (84th overall) and played for the Indianapolis Indians, the Pirates Triple-A club, as an outfielder during the 2014 season.

---

141 David Epstein, Op Cit.

Stan Belinda
August 6th 1994

The second, and final, pitcher in the '94 season to record a perfect inning was Stanley Peter Belinda. A right-handed reliever, Stan was born in Huntingdon, Pennsylvania on August 6th, 1966. Along with Trevor Wilson, he is the second and last pitcher in our list to record an immaculate inning on his birthday. Drafted by the Pittsburgh Pirates in the tenth round of the 1986 amateur draft, he made his debut with the Pirates on September 8th, 1989. Over a career that lasted twelve seasons, Belinda plated with six different Major League teams: Pirates (1989-93), Royals (1993-94), Red Sox (1995-96), Reds (1997-99), Rockies (2000) and Braves (2000). He made his final appearance in the Majors with the Braves on September 3rd, 2000. Belinda had a career 41-37 record, 4.15 ERA, 622 strikeouts, and 79 saves. He was described as a "side-arm" pitcher, who pitched with a three-quarter-arm slot. His fastball typically topped out in the low 90s and he also pitched a split-fingered fastball.[142] Most of his career was spent as a reliever, making only two professional appearances as a starter, both of which occurred in minor league games in '96 and '97.

Belinda's immaculate inning came in the 9th during a game against the visiting Seattle Mariners on August 6th, 1994. Pitching for the Royals, Belinda came on in the top of the inning with the goal of preventing any

---

142 James and Neyer, Op Cit, p.130

further damage, his team already down 11-2. He faced the bottom of the order: Eric Anthony, Chris Howard and Luis Sojo. Howard was caught looking on strike three, while both Anthony and Sojo struck out swinging. The Royals failed to score any runs in the bottom of the 9th and the Mariners claimed the win.

In 1998, while pitching for the Reds, Belinda complained of tingling sensations and numbness in his legs. He later received a diagnosis of multiple sclerosis (MS) while being a patient at the Mayo Clinic.[143] Copaxone, an immunomodulator drug used in the treatment of MS, coupled with changes to diet and lifestyle, allowed Belinda to play for two more seasons in the Majors. However, the effects of his disease were certainly evident in his stint with the Rockies; with an ERA over 7, he was released by Colorado in July of 2000. While he went on to sign with the Braves, he was eventually released in September of that season.

---

143 "Reds' Belinda Has Multiple Sclerosis," Associated Press in *LA Times* (September 22, 1998) reprinted in: http://articles.latimes.com/keyword/stan-belinda. Retrieved on October 11, 2014.

Todd Worrell
August 13th, 1995

For eleven seasons, Todd Worrell played the role of relief pitcher, first for the Cardinals (1985-1989, 1992) and later, the Dodgers (1993-1997). Todd Roland Worrell was born in Arcadia, California on September 28th, 1959. Drafted by the St. Louis Cardinals in the first round of the 1982 amateur player draft (21st pick overall), he made his first appearance in the Majors on August 28th, 1985, pitching in relief of Joaquin Andujar against the Reds. He went 1.2 innings, allowing no runs. A short time later, he picked up his first save on September 13th against the Cubs. The Cardinals made the postseason in 1985, in part because of the play of Worrell who recorded 5 saves in September, with an ERA of 2.91. Still in his rookie year, he would see post-season action against the Dodgers in the National League Championship and then the Royals in the 1985 World Series. Owing to his late start season, he was still eligible as a rookie in 1986; his continued effectiveness as a reliever (36 saves) would win him National League Rookie of the Year that season. He was also named the Rolaids Relief Man of the Year in '86.

In 1987, the Cardinals reached the post season again, ultimately facing the Minnesota Twins in the World Series. The Series would go to Game Seven in Minneapolis. Worrell came on in relief during the bottom of the 6th to hold the lead, with two Twins already on base. Worrell retired the first batter, but then walked Roy Smalley to load the bases. He then gave up a two-out RBI single to Greg Gagne. Worrell did not record the loss however, as the runner who scored was charged to the previous pitcher Danny Cox. The Twins would go on to win the game and the series.

By September, 1989, Worrell was on track to record his 125th career save, just one behind Bruce Sutter who held the record for the Cards. Injury, however, interceded and Worrell underwent Tommy John surgery in December. He subsequently missed both the '90 and '91 seasons rehabbing both shoulder and elbow injuries. While he returned to the Cards as set-up man for veteran reliever Lee Smith in '92, by December he had signed as a free agent with the Dodgers. Following a shaky couple of seasons in '93 and '94, Worrell found his way back to the kind of play that made him so memorable as a Cardinal. He recorded 111 saves from 1995 to 1997, and made the National League All-Star Team twice in back-to-back seasons (1995 and 1996). It was during this time that he also pitched a perfect inning for the Dodgers.

On August 13th, 1995, Worrell faced the bottom of the Pirate order (Mark Johnson, Angelo Encarnación and Steve Pegues) in the top of the 9th, having relieved Antonio Osuna. With his team up already by 3 runs, Worrell struck out Johnson and Encarnación swinging and then struck out Pegues looking. The Dodgers won, 4-1.

Shortly thereafter, Worrell officially retired from the Majors. He finished with a 50-52 record, 3.09 ERA, 628 strikeouts, and 256 saves. Commenting on Worrell's retirement, agent Rich Bry said: "The last couple of years Todd played, he told me that he knew the time was coming for him to be home with them (family) more. . . . He's putting the love for his family ahead of his love for the game now."[144] He was 38 years old when he finally called it a day.

---

144 Jason Reid, "Worrell Closes Door on Career," *LA Times* (Dec. 05, 1997): http://articles.latimes.com/1997/dec/05/sports/sp-61010 Retrieved on October 4, 2014

Mike Magnante
August 22nd, 1997

Michael Anthony Magnante was born on June 17th, 1965, in Glendale, California. A left-handed reliever, he played twelve seasons in the Majors for four different clubs: the Kansas City Royals (1991-96), Houston Astros (1997-98), Anaheim Angels (1999) and Oakland Athletics (2000-02). Mike was drafted by the Royals in the eleventh round of the 1988 amateur draft, and made his first appearance in the Majors on April 22nd, 1991. Magnante was known for three pitches: change-up, a fastball that typically topped-out in the low 80s, and a slider.[145] On July 29th, 2002, Magnante pitched his last game for the Oakland Athletics. His career statistics included a 26-32 win-loss record, 4.08 ERA and 347 strikeouts.

Magnante entered in the late innings of a game against the Colorado Rockies on August 22nd, 1997. After a scoreless 8th, Magnante returned to the mound for the top of the 9th to face Ellis Burks (batting in the 5th spot), Harvey Pulliam (who came in as a pinch hitter) and Jeff Reed. All three hitters were retired in order on nine pitches; all three struck-out swinging. The Astros won in a runaway 9-1 game, with Magnante pitching 2 innings in the game, allowing no hits, 1 base-on-balls and 4 strikeouts.

With the release of Michael Lewis' book and film-adaptation of *Moneyball*, Magnante was recently, and briefly, brought back into the limelight. Detailing

---

145 James and Neyer, Op Cit, p. 289.

the story of the 2002 Oakland A's under the leadership of GM Billy Beane, the film depicts the club's embrace of analytics as a means to improve the team's on-field performance. In terms of the pitchers discussed in the book and film, there is more of a focus on the acquisition of Ricardo Rincon. However, Magnante is also mentioned in both; the discrepancies between what is alleged about him in both, compared to first-person accounts, was the cause of some controversy. During the 2002 season, there was much tension between former A's manager Art Howe and Billy Beane, which later spilled into open conflict in the popular press following the release of the film. The story of Magnante's final days with the A's became just one of many points of contention in an open battle over whose version of events was correct. According to the story told in the movie, Billy Beane (played by Brad Pitt), was the person who told Magnante that he had been released by the A's. In fact, it was not Beane but Howe who delivered the bad news. According to Howe, he had to deliver the bad news knowing that Magnante was less than one week away from qualifying for his pension. "I like Mike, I tried hard to get him those days, I told them to put him on the DL (disabled list) to get him the time; it wouldn't have cost anything. They wouldn't."[146] In the book however, while it is acknowledged that Howe, not Beane, was the bearer of bad news for Magnante, the author had the timeline for the pitchers 10-year mark at four days away, and notes specifically that he would get his full pension even if they released him right away.[147] If Magnante was upset about the timing, he either didn't mention it to Lewis, or the author neglected to include it.

---

146 Will Braund, ""How True is Moneyball?" Late Innings: http://lateinnings.blogspot. ca/2012/03/how-true-is-moneyball.html. Retrieved on October 11, 2014.

147 Michael Lewis, *Moneyball: The Art of the Unfair Game*, W.W. Norton, 2004: p. 213.

Roger Clemens
September 18th, 1997

William "Roger" Clemens was born on August 4th, 1962, and played twenty-four seasons in the Majors, for four different ball clubs: the Boston Red Sox (1984-96), Toronto Blue Jays (1997-98), New York Yankees (1999-2003; 2007) and the Houston Astros (2004-06). As a Jays fan, I remember clearly when Clemens refused to re-sign with the Red Sox, and signed instead with Toronto. The deal was for four years at $40 million, and it certainly seemed at the time that the club was serious about putting a winning team on the field. Perhaps the best pitcher that club has ever had, he won the pitching Triple Crown twice and the Cy Young in his two seasons with Toronto.

Nicknamed the "Rocket", Clemens has been described as the essential power pitcher. While power is certainly essential in the modern game, it is difficult to be successful without control over the long term. There is a great story describing a young Clemens as not having enough power in his pitches to break a saltine cracker, but even in the early days, there was evidence that he had superb command.[148] Eventually, he learned to build power and speed from his back and legs. Together with his natural ability for control, Clemens' arsenal proved to be especially effective. Early in

---

148 Jeff Pearlman, *The Rocket that Feel to Earth: Roger Clemens and the Rage for Baseball Immortality*, Harper: New York, p. 21.

his career, he relied mostly on fastballs, often in the high 90s, and a hard breaking ball. Later, he developed a split-fingered fastball, which was used frequently with his fastball to play havoc with the timing of his opponents.

When he moved from Boston to Toronto, Clemens had lots of opportunity to face his old club with both being in the same division. It would be against the Red Sox, on September 18th, 1997, in the top of the 1st at Fenway, that Clemens would add an immaculate inning pitched to his impressive résumé. Facing the top of the order in Normar Garciaparra, John Valentin and Mo Vaughn, he dispatched these hitters on nine pitches—all called strikeouts. After the 5th, the score remained tied until the top of the 7th when Wakefield gave up a home run to Charlie O'Brien for the go-ahead run for the Jays. Paul Quantrill replaced Clemens in the bottom of the 8th and held the side to no runs. Boston though would break through again in the 9th and take the game, 3-2. Clemens finished the game having pitched 7 innings, allowing 1 run off 5 hits, while striking out 10 batters.

Clemens made his final appearance with the Yankees on September 16th, 2007. By that point in his career, the Rocket had been at the centre of a number of controversies in his professional and personal life. Part of this, most assuredly was the duality of the man, well-described and analyzed in the book, *The Rocket that Fell To Earth*. Simply put, Clemens' version of events, including his own biography, is a confabulation of truth and what he desired to be reality. On the diamond, he had a reputation for headhunting: pitching close, inside fastballs was his tendency, which greatly increased the likelihood of striking hitters. In 1995, he led the league in hit batsmen. Off the field, his infidelity became a news story. His reported love affair with country music singer Mindy McCready was especially newsworthy, owing to accusations the affair began when the singer was just 15 years old.[149] Arguably though, the most damaging to his reputation was accusations of steroid use. Clemens was named in both Jose Canseco's book, *Juiced: Wild Times, Rampant 'Roids, Smash Hits and How Baseball Got Big*, and in baseball's inquiry into performance-enhancing drugs, the *Mitchell Report*. Clemens denied the accusations publically, first on the news program 60 Minutes in January of 2008, and then again the next

---

149 Teri Thompson, Nathaniel Vinton and Christian Red, "Roger Clemens had 10-year fling with country star Mindy McCready," *New York Daily News*, (May 2, 2008) reprinted in: http://www.nydailynews.com/sports/baseball/yankees/sources-roger-clemens-10-year-fling-country-star-mindy-mccready-article-1.171271. Retrieved on December 27, 2014.

month in front of a Congressional committee.[150] By this point, he had already been convicted in the eyes of the public. His interpersonal style and his penchant for stretching the truth did not help his case. On August 19th, 2010, Clemens was indicted by a grand jury for perjury before Congress.[151] It would be two more years, on June 18th, 2012, before a decision of not guilty on all charges was declared.[152] Was Clemens vindicated? Not in the eyes of baseball writers voting for the Hall of Fame, as he has still not been voted into Cooperstown.

So far, the structure of these short essays has described the records and major achievements of the pitcher, usually in the opening or second paragraph. In light of the controversy over Clemens, and the on-going debate about his candidacy for the Hall, I have elected to have the last impression be about this remarkable pitcher's achievements, not his character. From his first appearance in the Majors on May 15th, 1984, he finished his career with a 354-184 record, 3.12 ERA and 4,672 strikeouts. Clemens was an eleven-time All-Star (1986, 1988, 1990-92, 1997-98, 2001, 2003-05) and part of two World Series teams (1999, 2000). A seven-time Cy Young Award winner (1986, 1987, 1991, 1997-98, 2001, 2004), he made history as the oldest pitcher to ever win the award. Clemens was also MVP for the American League in 1986, a two-time pitching Triple Crown winner (1997, 1998), seven-time ERA Champion (1986, 1990-92, 1997-98, 2005), five-time American League strikeout leader (1988, 1991, 1996-98) and four-time American League wins leader (1986-87, 1997-98). In 2006, he was named to *Sport Illustrated's* "all-time" team. Poignantly, he is the only pitcher who has recorded more than 300 wins and is not a member of the Hall of Fame.

---

150 "Clemens Vehemently Denies Steroid Use. Tells Mike Wallace Trainer Only Injected Legal Drug," CBS News (Jan. 03, 2008)" http://www.cbsnews.com/news/clemens-vehemently-denies-steroid-use/. Retrieved on December 14, 2014.

151 Dave Sheinin and Spencer S. Hsu, "Pitching legend Roger Clemens is indicted on charges of lying to a congressional committee," Washington Post (Aug. 20, 2010): http://www.washingtonpost.com/wp-dyn/content/article/2010/08/19/AR2010081904125_pf.html. Retrieved on December 14, 2014.

152 Juliet Macur, "Clemens Found Not Guilty of Lying About Drug Use," *New York Times* (June 12, 2012): http://www.nytimes.com/2012/06/19/sports/baseball/roger-clemens-is-found-not-guilty-in-perjury-trial.html?pagewanted=all&_r=0. Retrieved on December 27, 2014.

Doug Jones
September 23rd, 1997

Douglas Reid Jones was born in Covina, California on June 24th, 1957. A journeyman relief pitcher, Jones played sixteen seasons for six different clubs: the Milwaukee Brewers (1982, 1996-98), Cleveland Indians (1986-91, 1998), Phillies (1994), Orioles (1995), Chicago Cubs (1996), and Oakland As (1999-2000). Having attended Central Arizona College and Butler University in Indianapolis, he was drafted by the Brewers in the third round of the '78 amateur draft. Prior to his debut with that club on April 9th, 1982, and following a brief stint in the Majors (4 games), Jones spent seven years in the minors. His finished his career with a 69-79 record, 3.30 ERA, 909 strikeouts, and 303 saves over 846 games. Until 2006, he held the Indians' record for all-time saves at 129.

Jones relied on three pitches: slow fastball, change-up and screwball. He had a two-seam fastball that topped-out in the low to mid-80s, and mixed it with a screwball or knuckle curve. A noted change-up pitcher, his trademark approach was to throw increasingly slower and slower change-up pitches in succession, wreaking havoc on a hitter's timing.[153]

He was the last of three pitchers to pitch a perfect inning in 1997. On September 23rd, Jones faced Kansas City for the Brewers, coming on in the

---

153 "Doug Jones: Pitch Type," Fangraphs: http://www.fangraphs.com/statss. aspx?playerid=1006552&position=P. Retrieved on November 4, 2014.

9th to replace Alberto Reyes. He began by facing Johnny Damon, who was pinch-hitting for catcher Mike Macfarlane. Down by three runs, Damon struck out swinging on the third pitch. Jones then faced the top of the order in Scott Cooper and Rod Myers, and they were likewise dismissed on six pitches with Cooper swinging and Myers caught looking. Jones would receive the save, Reyes the win, and the Brewers won the contest 7-4.

After a long career, Jones retired at the age of 43 in 2000. His last appearance was on September 29th for the Oakland As. A resident of Tucson Arizona, Jones splits his time between being an assistant coach for the San Diego Christian College Hawks and running a Christian music recording label with his wife.[154]

---

154 Greg Popelka, "Cleveland Indians Closer Doug Jones – Reliving Yesteryear," Waiting For Next Year: http://www.waitingfornextyear.com/2014/08/cleveland-indians-closer-doug-jones-reliving-yesteryear/. Retrieved on November 4, 2014.

Jimmy Key
April 14th, 1998

I used to own a Blue Jays baseball cap signed by Jimmy Key. I don't recall exactly how old I was or the precise circumstances surrounding how I got it, but it would have been in the in mid- to late 80s, and it was a gift from my older brother. He was a manager with Zellers at the time, a Canadian retail company that had a sponsorship deal with the Jays, and I recall he got it from Key at some corporate meet and greet. I no longer have it, which I sincerely regret. Jimmy Key was an important part of that Blue Jays in the late '80s and early '90s, and he is certainly in the conversation when discussing the best pitchers in Jays history.

James Edward "Jimmy" Key was born on April 22nd, 1961, in Huntsville, Alabama. He began his pitching career at S.R. Butler High School in Huntsville, where he had a 10-0 record and a 0.30 ERA in his senior year (his batting average was no joke either at .410). He continued his dominating performance as both a pitcher and batter for the Clemson Tigers, posting a 2.79 ERA and a .300 batting average. In 1982, Key was selected by the Toronto Blue Jays during the third round of the amateur draft. He made his first appearance with that club on April 6th, 1984. Throughout his fifteen-season career, Jimmy would play for a total of three cubs, all in the American League East division: Toronto Blue Jays (1984-92), New York Yankees (1993-96) and the Baltimore Orioles (1997-98). A four-time All-Star (1985, 1991, 1993, 1994), he played on two World Series Teams

(Jays in 1992 and the Yankees in 1996) and led the American League in wins during the shortened strike season of 1994. He was also the American League ERA leader in 1987, posting a 2.76.[155] A leftie, Key was known for four pitches: a curve, fastball, change-up and slider.[156] Although his fastball lacked the velocity that many of his contemporaries had, he had excellent control and could spot the ball well on the corners.

For Jays fans, Key will be best remembered for his post-season appearances for Toronto. Particularly memorable was Game Four of the 1992 World Series. Not only did Key get the win, pitching 7.2 innings allowing only 1 run off 5 hits, he also showcased one of his truly special talents, by picking off Otis Nixon in the top of the 1st inning. Nixon stole 41 bases in the regular season in 1991, five against Toronto in the postseason alone.[157] According to Key, "I was very fortunate in the first inning. I got the ball up and I was a little concerned. When I have trouble, it's usually early. They hit the ball hard but right at people. I was fortunate to pick off Otis. After that, I got my feet on the ground and pitched my game the rest of the time I was out there."[158] That win would put the Jays up 3-1 in the Series. However, a Braves' win in Game Five created the opportunity for Key to make another appearance in the Series. This time he came in as a reliever in the 10th and 11th innings of Game Six. Key got the win again, holding the Braves to just 2 runs. Dave Winfield doubled in the top of the 11th, scoring Devon White and Roberto Alomar, and the Jays won the game and the Series, their first of what would be back-to-back World Series wins in '92 and '93.

Jimmy Key's final game in the Majors was as a Baltimore Oriole on September 20th, 1998. That same season, he added one more record to his résumé: pitching a perfect inning. Early in the 1998 campaign, on April 14th, 1998, Key took the mound to face the Chicago White Sox at home in Camden Yards. In the top of the 2nd, facing the 5th, 6th and 7th batters in the lineup, Key retired Robin Ventura, Magglio Ordóñez, and Ray Durham

155 Baseball Reference: http://www.baseball-reference.com/players/k/keyji01.shtml. Retrieved on November 2, 2014.

156 James and Neyer, Op Cit, p.265.

157 Baseball Reference: http://www.baseball-reference.com/players/n/nixonot01.shtml. Retrieved on November 2, 2014.

158 Murray Chass, "World Series - Key Brings the Blue Jays Just One Game Away," *New York Times* (Oct. 22, 1992):. http://www.nytimes.com/1992/10/22/sports/world-series-key-brings-the-blue-jays-just-one-game-away.html. Retrieved on November 2, 2014.

in order on nine pitches. All struck out swinging. Key himself notched the win, pitching 7 innings and allowing just 1 run on 3 hits, while striking out 7. The Orioles defeated the White Sox, 4-3.

Key had his fair share of injuries, including surgery to remove bone chips in his elbow in 1988. While these may have affected his career numbers in baseball, they did not seem to hurt his golf game. He is known, at least in some circles, to be a decent amateur golfer.[159]

---

159 Tom Dakers, "Top 50 All-Time Jays: #7 Jimmy Key," SB Nation: http://www. bluebirdbanter.com/2009/5/11/872139/top-50-all-time-jays-7-jimmy-key. Retrieved on November 7, 2014.

Mike Mussina
May 9th, 1998

Michael Cole Mussina (nicknamed "Moose") was the second pitcher in the 1998 season to pitch a perfect inning. From his first appearance in 1991 to his last on September 28th, 2008, Mussina racked-up a number of impressive achievements as a member of both the Baltimore Orioles and the New York Yankees. He was a five-time All-Star (1992-94, 1997, 1999), a seven-time Gold Glove winner (1996-1999, 2001, 2003, 2008) and the American League Wins leader in 1995. Additionally, Mussina was part of the 2001 and 2003 World Series winning Yankee teams, and 20-game winner in his final year in the Majors. These accolades and accomplishments make it is easy to see why a case can be made for Mussina to be in the Hall of Fame. At the same time, it is easy to forget these achievements when Mussina is equally renowned for his list of missed opportunities and runner-up finishes. Consider the following: Mussina was in the top five in voting for the Cy Young award six times, but never won the top honour. In six starts from 1992 to 2004, Mussina came close to pitching a perfect game but was foiled each time. In 1997, in a game against the Cleveland Indians, he retired 25 batters before giving up a single to Sandy Alomar Jr. in the 9th. He finished the game though with an impressive one-hit shut-out. The following season, he again retired 23 batters in a game against the Tigers but surrendered a double to Frank Catalanotto in the last of the 8th inning. The game finished with another shutout win for Mussina.

Born on December 8th, 1968 in Williamsport, Pennsylvania, Mike Mussina began his pitching career for the Montoursville Area High School, where he recorded a 24-4 record and an ERA under 1. Although drafted out of high school by the Orioles in 1987, he opted instead for college. While attending Stanford University, he played three seasons compiling a 31-16 record with a 3.89 ERA. Still interested in Mussina, the Orioles drafted the star prospect in the first round of the 1990 amateur draft (20th pick overall). Mussina was known to have a rich arsenal of seven pitches: a two-seam and four-seam fastball, a knuckle curve, a cut fastball, an overhand curve, a change-up and a slider. His knuckle curve was thrown by flicking the ball out of his hand.[160] It is easy to see why Mussina was so successful for so long. His excellent control and ability to adjust with so many pitches at his disposal gave him the tools to succeed. Mussina played in the Majors for 18 years, retiring with a 270-153 record, 3.68 ERA and 2,813 strikeouts.

On May 9th, 1998, just about a month after fellow Oriole Jimmy Key pitched his perfect inning, Mussina added an immaculate inning to his career record. The opposing team was the Tampa Bay Rays, in an evening game at the Trop. Having pitched all 8 innings and denying the Rays any runs, Mussina took the mound in the bottom of the 9th to face the middle of the order in Fred McGriff, Paul Sorrento, and Rich Butler. Both McGriff and Butler struck out swinging, while Sorrento was caught looking. A complete game in the books, Mussina's shutout win was truly impressive, having allowed just 5 hits and no walks while striking out 10 in a 7-0 pasting. Completing the outing with an immaculate inning was a truly a poignant finish to an already impressive evening of pitching.

Though the '98 season included two different pitchers from the same team throwing back-to-back immaculate innings, these highlights were two of the very few over an otherwise underwhelming year. With the likes of Cal Ripken Jr., Rafael Palmeiro and Roberto Alomar in the infield, along with Key and Mussina in the starting rotation, the '98 Orioles were dubbed "ancient and falling apart" at the start of the season and lived up to the billing when they ultimately finished under .500 for the season.[161]

---

160 James and Neyer, Op Cit, p. 319.

161 Thomas Boswell, "Orioles Rush to Judgment Over Slow Start," *Los Angeles Times* (May 09, 1998): http://articles.latimes.com/1998/may/09/sports/sp-48005. Retrieved on November 22, 2014.

As for Mussina, he retired to his hometown and is an active member of the local community, coaching youth sport. The debate over his Hall of Fame candidacy will undoubtedly continue, but in addition to the points raised earlier, he faces formidable competition as numerous worthy candidates come up for nomination each year and other controversial candidates from the steroid era clog the ballot.

Orel Hershiser
June 16th, 1998

Orel Hershiser was born in Buffalo, New York, on September 16th, 1958. He was drafted in the seventeenth round of the '79 draft by the Los Angeles Dodgers, having played college ball before that at Bowling Green State University. He made his first appearance in the Majors on September 1st, 1983, for the Dodgers. From there, he went on to have a very successful career, lasting eighteen seasons in the Majors with four different teams: the Los Angeles Dodgers (1983-94, 2000), Cleveland Indians (1995-97), San Francisco Giants (1998) and the New York Mets (1999). His career numbers include a 204-150 record, 3.48 ERA, and 2,014 strikeouts. He was named to the All-Star Team three times (1987-89), won the World Series with the Dodgers in 1988 and was the Series MVP in '88. That same year he won the 1988 National League Cy Young Award and was also twice-named the League Championship Series MVP in 1988 and 1995.

Hershiser had four pitches: a sinker, cut fastball, curve and straight change-up. By his own account, his curves had three different speeds and angles. His straight change had the arm action of a fastball, but the difference was the grip and release, which was just enough to reduce the speed to trick batters into believing a fastball was coming, causing no end of trouble to their timing.[162]

---

162 James and Neyer, Op Cit, p. 241

On June 16th, 1998, Hershiser's Giants took the field to face the Colorado Rockies. In the top of the 1st, Hershiser induced three groundouts to retire the top of the order in the Rockies line-up. A tie game in the 4th, Hershiser struck out Ellis Burks, Vinny Castilla, and Todd Helton. Three up, three down on a total of nine pitches. However, after his immaculate inning, Hershiser got roughed up in the 6th and was eventually replaced by Marvin Benard the following inning. The Giants rallied back in the bottom of the 7th, scoring 3 runs, and ultimately winning 5-3. Hershiser pitched 6.1 innings, allowing 3 runs off 8 hits. He struck out 5 batters and walked 2.

Among the many notable moments in his long career was his streak of consecutive scoreless innings. It began on August 30th, 1988 in a game against the Montreal Expos, and ended on April 5th, 1989 in a game against the Cincinnati Reds. During that time, he pitched 59 innings allowing no runs and thereby breaking the previous record of 58 set by Don Drysdale in 1968. Drysdale was the radio announcer for the Dodgers at the time and actually called some of the games during the streak.

Hershiser played his final game for the club that drafted him on June 26th, 2000. On his first year of eligibility for the Hall of Fame in 2006, he received 14% of the vote, far short of the number needed for entry. In 2007 however, he was eliminated from the ballot after he only received 4.4% of the total votes. Hershiser faced stiff competition, as both Cal Ripken and Tony Gwynn were elected on their first ballots that year, and Jim Rice, Andre Dawson, Bert Blyleven and Rich Gossage all received solid totals and eventually were elected to the Hall. Outside of baseball, Hershiser worked for the both the Dodgers and ESPN as a colour commentator. Hershiser has also had success as an amateur poker player. Given his current interests on the felt, it is perhaps not surprising that he lives in Las Vegas with his second wife and her two children.

Randy Johnson
September 2ⁿᵈ, 1998 & August 23ʳᵈ, 2001

Randall David "Randy" Johnson was the fourth pitcher, and to date the last, to pitch more than one immaculate inning. The left-handed "Big Unit", as he was known by fans and foes alike, was truly an impressive and intimating figure on the mound. At 6'10", Johnson held the record for tallest player in the Majors for most of his long career. He played twenty-two seasons in the big leagues on six different ball clubs: the Montreal Expos (1988-89), Seattle Mariners (1989-98), Houston Astros (1998), Arizona Diamondbacks (1999-2004; 2007-08), New York Yankees (2005-06), and San Francisco Giants (2009). Born on September 10th, 1963, in Walnut Creek, California, he was drafted by the Expos in the second round of the '85 amateur draft, and made his debut on September 15th, 1988, at the age of 25. Like so many of the great pitchers in this collection, his career record includes an almost exhausting list of accomplishments. He was an All-Star ten times over his career (1990, 1993-95, 1997, 1999-2002, 2004); a World Series Champion and MVP in 2001 with the Diamondbacks; a five-time Cy Young Award Winner (1995, 1999-2002). Johnson also won the pitching Triple Crown in 2002, the same year he led the National League in wins. Four times he was league-leader in ERA (1995, 1999, 2001, 2002), and nine-times he was the Strikeout leader (1992-1995, 1999-2002, 2004). He pitched a no-hitter on June 2ⁿᵈ, 1990 against the Detroit Tigers. On May 18th, 2004, he pitched a perfect game against the Atlanta

Braves, becoming just the seventeenth pitcher in Major League history to do so. He was the fifth pitcher in Major League history to pitch no-hitters in both leagues (along with Cy Young, Jim Bunning, Nolan Ryan and Hideo Nomo).[163] In 2015, Johnson was elected to the Hall of Fame on his first ballot.

Like so many pitchers who had long careers, Johnson's pitch selection changed over time. In the early 1990s, he was known for three pitches: a fastball in the high 90s, a sharp curve and a change-up. In the mid- to late 1990s, he relied more on a mid-90s fastball and a hard slider. Johnson had a three-quarter arm delivery and is well-remembered for his high velocity fastballs, which often reached speeds in excess of 100 mph. His sliders also frequently reached the low 90s.

Johnson's first recorded immaculate inning occurred on September 2nd, 1998, in a game against the Atlanta Braves. Johnson faced off against fellow ace Greg Maddux at Turner Field. In the bottom of the 6th, Johnson faced the middle of the Braves' lineup: Javy Lopez, Andruw Jones, and Greg Colbrunn. At this point, his club was already ahead by 2 runs. Lopez took strike three looking, while both Jones and Colbrunn swung and missed for strike three. The Astros went on to win 4-2, with Johnson allowing just 1 run off 4 hits over 8 innings, striking out a total of 10 batters and walking 3.

The 6th inning proved to lucky for Johnson again, at least in relation to immaculate innings, when he pitched his second immaculate on August 23rd, 2001. Pitching for the Diamondbacks, Johnson took the field to face the Pirates at PNC Park. In the middle of a pitchers' duel with the Pirates' Tony McKnight, Johnson took the mound in the bottom of the 6th. Facing the number nine and top two batters in the lineup, Johnson repeated his perfect performance of 1998 and retired all three batters on just nine pitches. McKnight, who was batting in the number nine spot, was retired looking at strike three, while Gary Matthews went looking and Jack Wilson struck out swinging. The bottom of the 7th, however, would not be kind to the Big Unit, as he surrendered 4 runs before finally leaving the game. The Pirates eventually won, 5-1. While Johnson recorded an impressive 16 strikeouts, he also gave up 4 earned runs off just 5 hits over 7 innings.

---

163 "Randy Johnson Player Page," Baseball Reference: http://www.baseball-reference. com/players/j/johnsra05.shtml. Retrieved on December 20, 2014.

In March 2001, during a game against the San Francisco Giants, Johnson struck and killed a dove, whose flight path happened regrettably to intersect with one of his deliveries. Onlookers described the impact as an explosion of feathers. His catcher that day, Rod Barajas, recalled: "I'm sitting there waiting for it (the ball), and I'm expecting to catch the thing, and all you see is an explosion. It's crazy. There's still feathers down there."[164] Although many of the Giants were amused and teased the big man, Johnson simply commented that he didn't feel it was very funny. As surly and fierce on the field as he was, Johnson was not completely devoid of a sense of humor. He appeared as a guest star on the *Simpsons*, and starred in an amusing men's deodorant commercial where he played himself hurling fireballs at Kyle Brandt, who was playing the role of 'body odor.'

164 "Randy Johnson Kills Dove with Pitch," ABC News (March 26, 2001): http://abcnews.go.com/Sports/story?id=99757. Retrieved on December 20, 2014.

Jesus Sanchez
September 13ᵗʰ, 1998

Jesus Paulino Sanchez was born in Nizao, Dominican Republic on October 11ᵗʰ, 1974. He played for four different clubs in the Majors over seven seasons: the Florida Marlins (1998-2001), Chicago Cubs (2002), Colorado Rockies (2003) and Cincinnati Reds (2004). Drafted as an amateur free agent by the Mets in 1992, he made his first appearance with the Marlins on March 31ˢᵗ, 1998. Over his career, Sanchez had a 23-34 record, 5.32 ERA, and 384 strikeouts. A left-handed pitcher, his numbers from 2002 to 2004 show he relied mainly on his fastball (66% of the time), then slider (18%), change-up (14%) and curve ball (2%).

On September 13ᵗʰ, 1998, as a pitcher for the Marlins, Sanchez pitched a perfect inning against the Atlanta Braves at Turner Field. Sanchez was the starting pitcher; in the bottom of the 3ʳᵈ inning, he took the mound to face: Tony Graffanino, Greg Maddux, and Walt Weiss. All three struck out swinging. Sanchez eventually pitched seven solid innings and beat the Braves 6-5. He notched the win, giving up 5 earned runs on 5 hits, while striking out 10 batters. The key to his success was his curve ball: "Last year in Double-A, they asked me why I didn't throw a curve ball, I told them it's because I have a good slider."[165] The curve was just fine that day though.

---

165 "Marlins Stop Braves Celebration," CBS News (Sept 13, 1998): http://www.cbsnews.com/news/marlins-stop-braves-celebration/. Retrieved on November 4, 2014.

Sanchez played his last game, for the Cincinnati Reds, on July 15th, 2004. He continued to play ball after he finished in the Majors though, most recently playing for the York Revolution in the Atlantic League in 2012.

Shane Reynolds
July 15ᵗʰ, 1999

Born on March 26ᵗʰ, 1968, in Bastrop, Louisiana, Richard Shane Reynolds was one of two pitchers to record an immaculate inning in the 1999 season. A righted-handed starter, Reynolds played thirteen seasons in the big leagues with the Houston Astros (1992-2002), Atlanta Braves (2003) and Arizona Diamondbacks (2004). Drafted in the third round of the amateur draft in 1989 by the Astros, Reynolds made his debut on July 20ᵗʰ, 1992. Like so many before and after him, Reynolds played both high school and university ball. He was a three-time All-State selection and a two-time Big 12 First-Team selection while attending the University of Texas. An All-Star in 2000, his career stats include a 114-96 record, 4.09 ERA, and 1,403 strikeouts. Reynolds best years came with the Astros. Between 1998 and '99, he went 35-22, with a 3.66 ERA over 70 games. Reynolds had three pitches: a split-fingered fastball, fastball and curve.[166] Hall of Fame pitcher Greg Maddux had this to say about his stuff: "When his control is good, you can't pitch any better. You've got to do two things to pitch. You've got to locate your fastball and change speeds. He's got a very good fastball and he's great at changing his speeds. When he can locate his fastball, he's almost unhittable."[167]

---

166 James and Neyer, Op Cit., p.357.

167 Louisiana Sports of Hall of Fame: http://www.lasportshall.com/inductees/baseball/shane-reynolds/?back=inductee. Retrieved on November 4, 2014.

On July 15th, 1999, Reynolds took the mound to face a struggling Detroit Tigers team (36-53 at that point in the season). In the top of the 1st, facing the top of the order, Reynolds struck out Juan Encarnación, Brad Ausmus and Bobby Higginson on just nine pitches. Encarnación struck out looking, while both Ausmus and Higginson struck out swinging. The rest of the game would not go so well for Reynolds, as he left the game after the 5th, having given up 8 hits and 6 earned runs. Luckily, the Astros offence made up the difference and won 8-6.

By 2003, Reynolds' ERA was up over 5, though he still managed to win 11 games for the Braves. He retired in 2004 after an injury kept him out of most of the season. He was inducted into the Louisiana Sport Hall of Fame in 2014.[168]

---

168 Op. cit.

B.J. Ryan
September 5th, 1999

Robert Victor "B.J." Ryan, Jr., is best known for his time as a relief pitcher with the Toronto Blue Jays. Born on December 28th, 1975, in Bossier City, Louisiana, he was drafted in the seventeenth round in the 1998 amateur draft by the Cincinnati Reds and made his debut on July 28th, 1999. He attended the University of Louisiana, prior to being drafted into the Majors.[169] Ryan never officially retired from the game (at least to the time of writing of this book), even though he has not played since July 5th, 2009, with the Jays.

Ryan had an interesting three-quarter throwing action, described as a slingshot-like delivery that proved especially effective against left-handed batters. In his prime, he could get his fastball (typically in the low 90s) to tail off at the plate. When added to an arsenal that included a slider, Ryan had reasonably good success pitching against right-handed batters. However, struggles with command ensured his career would be limited to the bullpen. He has a 21-28 record, 3.37 ERA, 625 strikeouts and 117 saves.

On September 5th, 1999, in front of more than 44,000 fans at Camden Yards in Baltimore, Ryan, pitching for the Orioles, relieved Sidney Ponson in the top of the 5th inning. The bases were loaded, Ponson having walked the

---

169 "BJ Ryan Player Page,", Baseball Reference: http://www.baseball-reference.com/players/r/ryanb.01.shtml. Retrieved on September 10, 2014.

first three batters. With his club up 7-5, Ryan had a horrendous outing; allowing a total of 7 runs before ending the inning. However, Ryan remained in the game for the top of the 6th, and was perfect. Facing the heart of the Indians lineup, Ryan fanned Manny Ramirez, Jim Thome and Richie Sexson on nine pitchers. The Orioles ended up losing the game, 15-7. Despite a perfect 6th, Ryan's numbers were not pretty (thanks in large part to Ponson): in just 2 innings, he gave up 4 earned hits on 3 hits.

In addition to his perfect inning, Ryan's time with the Orioles is marked with another rare achievement: winning a game without actually throwing a pitch. On May 1st, 2003, Ryan's first and only throw in the game was a pick-off to first base, successfully catching Omar Infante on a steal attempt for the last out. The Orioles took the lead in the next inning, scoring 3 runs in the top of the 8th. Ryan was relieved by Buddy Groom in the 9th, but as the pitcher of record he was given the win.

Ryan's final year with Baltimore, and his subsequent move to Toronto, proved to be his most productive (2004 to 2006). With Baltimore in '04, Ryan transitioned from the club's set-up man to replace Jorge Julio as the team's closer. Ryan was able to parlay his success with the Orioles in that season to become one of the most sought-after free agents in the Majors during the 2005 off-season. Blue Jays fans will remember the landmark contract General Manager, J.P. Ricciardi gave Ryan only too well. Turning down offers from the Orioles, Indians and the Yankees, Ryan signed a five-year, $4 million contract with the Jays, surpassing the previous record for a contract to a reliever held by Mariano Rivera when he signed with the Yankees at 4-years, $39.99 million. Initially, the deal began well. In 2005, Ryan had arguably his best year, posting a 2.43 ERA, coupled with an 87% save opportunities conversion (36 of 41). He was also named to the American League All-Star Team. Ryan also had a very successful 2006 with the Jays, recording a 1.37 ERA and a save conversion percentage of 90% (38 for 42). However, it was after 2006 that Ryan's deal with the Jays turned sour. By May, 2007, Ray underwent Tommy John surgery and never again came close to his best numbers. In July of 2009, the Jays released him. Riccardi had only this to say: "we just don't think he's going to be the pitcher he was when we signed him."[170] The club still owed Ryan $15 million on his contract when they parted ways.

---

170 Riccardi quoted in "Blue Jays Release BJ Ryan," CBC Sports (July 8th, 2009): http://www.cbc.ca/sports/baseball/blue-jays-release-b-j-ryan-1.790269. Retrieved on October 3, 2014.

The Chicago Cubs signed Ryan just eight days after his release from Jays: however, he never played for the Cubs or for their Triple-A affiliate Iowa. He was granted an unconditional release on August 5th, 2009.

PART V: 2000-2014

Ugueth Urbina
April 4th, 2000

The first pitcher of the new millennium to record a perfect inning, and the only one in the 2000 season, was Ugueth Urtain Urbina Villarreal. Born on February 15th, 1974, the Venezuelan relief pitcher played eleven seasons in the Majors for six different clubs: the Montreal Expos (1995-2001), Red Sox (2001-02), Texas Rangers (2003), Florida Marlins (2003), Detroit Tigers (2004-05) and Philadelphia Phillies (2005). Signed by the Montreal Expos as an amateur free agent in 1990, Urbina made his Major League debut on May 9th, 1995, at the age of 21. His longest and arguably most successful stint in the Majors was with the Expos. In 1999, he led the National League with 41 saves and posted a 3.69 ERA over 71 games. He also made the All-Star Team twice in 1998 and 2002. After leaving that club, and following brief periods with Boston and the Texas Rangers, Urbina played for the World Series Champion Marlins in 2003. While only with the team for a short period, having been traded from the Rangers in July, Urbina appeared in ten games in the postseason, going 1-0 with 3.46 ERA and 4 saves. Over eleven seasons, Urbina finished with a 44-49 record, 3.45 ERA, 814 strikeouts and 237 saves. His final game was on October 2nd, 2005, for the Phillies, and the circumstances behind his departure were anything but ordinary.

On April 4th, 2000, Urbina became the forty-ninth pitcher, and third Montreal Expo, to pitch an immaculate inning. Facing the Los Angeles

Dodgers, Urbina entered the game in the top of the 9th, replacing first basemen Lee Stevens. Facing the number nine hitter Frank Paul Santangelo, Urbina retired him on three pitches, with a swinging third strike. Moving on to the top of the order with Devon White and Mark Grudzielanek, Urbina fanned both swinging. Although Urbina allowed no runs, his club was already behind by 6. Failing to score any runs in the bottom of the 9th, the Expos lost 10-4. In spite of his first appearance of the year, Urbina's '00 season proved to be a rough one, as he only made thirteen appearances due to injury.

Despite what might otherwise be described as a respectable career as a closer, Urbina will likely be remembered for events that occurred outside the game. In the span of just over fourteen months, two strange events would precede Urbina's eventual departure from the game. First, in September, 2004, Urbina's mother, Maura Villarreal, was kidnapped and held for ransom in Venezuela. The kidnappers demanded a $6 million ransom from the family. They flatly refused, and it would be more than five months before the 54-year-old Maura was rescued. In dramatic fashion, Venezuelan police stormed an abandoned tourist mountain camp near the Guaniamo River, some 340 miles southwest of Caracas. While most of her abductors were able to escape, one was killed in a shootout with police.[171] Sadly, this was not the first (or last) instance of violence that touched the Villarreal family: Urbina's father had been killed ten years earlier during a failed robbery attempt.

In 2005, just a few months after his mother was rescued, Urbina would again come into contact with Venezuelan authorities, this time as a perpetrator not a victim. On October 16th, Urbina attacked five farm workers on his property, allegedly over a stolen gun. By one account, Urbina attacked the men first with a machete, and then by pouring gasoline over them in an attempt to set them on fire.[172] On March 28th, he was sentenced to fourteen years for attempted murder. He would serve more than five years before being released just before Christmas in 2012. Ranking in the top fifty

---

171 "At least one abductor killed in rescue mission," Associated Press reprinted in ESPN.com (Feb. 19, 2005): http://sports.espn.go.com/mlb/news/story?id=1994812. Retrieved on October 30, 2014.

172 "Baseball Round-up: Urbina Given 14 Years For Attempted Murder," *New York Times* (March 29, 2007) reprinted in: http://query.nytimes.com/gst/fullpage. html?res=9901EEDD1030F93AA15750C0A9619C8B63&scp=2&sq=Ugueth%20 Urbina&st=cse. Retrieved on October 30, 2014.

crooked athletes in sports history, the Bleacher Report placed Urbina eighteenth overall.[173] It may not be entirely fair to judge Urbina without a least considering the environment in which he and his family live. Racked by violence, Venezuela was ranked by a 2013 Gallup Poll as the most insecure nation in the world to live, with the second highest murder rate anywhere.[174] While I am not condoning his actions, it is a tragic fact that violence is a fact of everyday life for many who live in that troubled country.

---

173 Ethan Norof, "50 Most Crooked Athletes in Sports History," Bleacher Report (July 13, 2011): http://bleacherreport.com/articles/765105-50-most-crooked-athletes-in-sports-history/page/34. Retrieved on October 30, 2014.

174 "Latin America Scores Lowest on Security. Venezuelans report lowest security levels worldwide," Gallup: http://www.gallup.com/poll/175082/latin-america-scores-lowest-security.aspx. Retrieved on December 2, 2014.

Jason Isringhausen
April 13th, 2002

Jason Derek Isringhausen was the first of four pitchers to record a perfect inning in the 2002 season. Born in Brighton Illinois on September 7th, 1972, Isringhausen pitched in the Majors from 1995 through 2012 for five different clubs: the New York Mets (1995-97, 1999, 2011), Oakland A's (1999-2001), St. Louis Cardinals (2002-08), Tampa Bay Rays (2009) and Angels (2012). Drafted in the forty-fourth round by the Mets in the '91 amateur draft, Isringhausen, Bill Pulsipher and Paul Wilson comprised a trio of highly touted Mets prospects dubbed "Generation K." Isringhausen ultimately did not make it as a starter and eventually found his home in the bullpen. His career numbers included a 51-55 record, a 3.64 ERA, 830 strikeouts and 300 saves. He was named to the All-Star Team twice (2000 and 2005) and in 2004 led the National League with 47 saves. A 6'3", 230 lb. right-hander, Isringhausen's scouting report included a fastball, typically in the mid-90s, a cut fastball and a curveball.[175] While he principally relied on his fastball, he also used a slider, cutter, an occasional change-up, and, very rarely, a split-fingered fastball.[176]

On April 13th, 2002, playing for the Cardinals, Isringhausen came into a tight 1-1 game in the 9th against the Astros. Facing Daryle Ward, José

---

175 James and Neyer, Op Cit., p.253.

176 "Jason Isringhausen," FanGraphs:http://www.fangraphs.com/statss.aspx?playerid=1158 &position=P. Retrieved on November 4, 2014.

Vizcaíno, and Julio Lugo, Isringhausen struck out all three on nine pitches. All three batters went down swinging. In the bottom of that inning, Eli Marrero drove in the winning run and the Cards won, 2-1. Isringhausen received the win.

Isringhausen's career was plagued with injuries, a mixture of overuse during the season, bad judgment and bad luck. He had three surgeries to his pitching arm, broke his wrist punching a garbage can in the dugout and suffered tuberculosis. After he retired, Isringhausen served as a volunteer coach at Southern Illinois University in Edwardsville.

Byung-Hyun Kim
May 11th, 2002

Byung-Hyun Kim is the only South Korean pitcher to record a perfect inning in the Majors. Born on January 19th, 1979, Kim signed as an amateur free agent with the Arizona Diamondbacks in 1999, making his Major League debut on May 29th of that same year. From 1999 to 2007, Kim played for four different clubs: the Diamondbacks (1999-2003, 2007), Boston Red Sox (2003-04), Colorado Rockies (2005-07), and Florida Marlins (2007). During his career, he had several notable achievements including being named an All-Star (2002) and playing for two World Series Championship teams (2001 Diamondbacks and 2004 Red Sox). In 2006, Kim was selected for the South Korean squad at the World Baseball Classic. His last appearance in the Majors was with the Marlins on September 28th, 2007. Over his career, he posted a 54-60 record, 4.42 ERA, 806 strikeouts, and 86 saves.

Kim was a right-handed submarine, or side-arm, pitcher. He relied mostly on his fastball (about 64% of the time), slider (28%) and change-up (8%). A former teammate described Kim's stuff: "He has the filthiest slider to a right-hander in baseball when he's on. It never stops breaking. And his 90-mph fastball from the down-under angle keeps hitters honest."[177]

---

177 Jayson Stark, "The pitches that scare major leaguers,"ESPN.com: http://static.espn. go.com/mlb/columns/stark_jayson/1382666.html. Retrieved on December 2, 2014.

Kim's immaculate inning occurred on May 11th, 2002, in a game against the Phillies at Veterans Stadium. The Diamondbacks were ahead by one run in the bottom of the 8th, when Kim entered the game to replace Damian Miller. Facing the middle of the order in Scott Rolen, Mike Lieberthal and Pat Burrell, Kim retired the side on nine pitches with both Rolen and Lieberthal striking out swinging. Kim took the mound again in the 9th inning to protect a slim 1-run lead, however he conceded a 1-out home run that forced the game into extra innings. After the Diamondbacks scored a run in the top of the 10th, Kim finished the game to secure the win. In three innings pitched, Kim allowed 2 hits, 1 home run, no walks and 4 strikeouts. The Diamondbacks won the game, 6-5.

Kim is probably best remembered for his post-season appearances with the Diamondbacks and Red Sox. In his first appearance, during Game Three of the 2001 National League Division Series against the Cardinals, Kim entered the game in the 8th and kept his team ahead 5-3, ultimately earning the save on a game-ending double play off Mark McGwire. In the National League Championship Series, he picked up two more saves in Games Four and Five, securing a trip to the World Series. However, his successes would not be repeated in the World Series. In his first appearance in Game Four, coming in relief of Curt Schilling in the 8th with the DBacks up by 2, he eventually gave up the lead in the 9th inning, and ultimately took the loss. In Game Five, he again gave up a 9th inning lead by surrendering a two-run homer off Tino Martinez that ultimately led to a loss for the Diamondbacks in extra innings. Despite his performance, the Diamondbacks went on to win the World Series in seven games. Kim again tasted postseason play with the Red Sox in 2004. His only appearance came in Game One of the American League Division Series, where his lack of success with hitters that day led to him being pulled in the 9th with 2 outs. In his next appearance in Game Three, Red Sox fans at Fenway let Kim know what they thought about his previous performance: he was booed soundly during lineup introductions. Kim let fans know how he felt with a middle-finger salute.[178]

As of writing, the 35 year-old pitcher was still playing professional baseball. In 2014, he was a member of the starting rotation for the KIA Tigers, a pro team in the Korean Baseball Organization.

---

178 "Kim Apologizes for Gesture," Associated Press reprinted in ESPN.com: http://sports. espn.go.com/mlb/playoffs2003/news/story?id=1630608. Retrieved December on 2, 2014.

Pedro Martínez
May 18th, 2002

A mere seven days after Kim's immaculate feat, the third pitcher in '02 to record a perfect inning was none other than Pedro Martínez. Dominican born, the powerful, yet somewhat diminutive (5'11"), right-hander had a long and productive career in the Majors. He played for five different clubs including the Dodgers (1992-93), Expos (1994-97), Red Sox (1998-2004), Mets (2005-08) and Phillies (2009). Born on October 25th, 1971, Martínez signed as an amateur free agent in 1988, making his debut with LA as a September call up in 1992. His pitching style has been described as a three-quarter, almost sidearm, delivery. He commanded five different pitches: hard curve, fastball, sinking fastball, slider and change-up. What made him particularly effective was both his ability to shift between a blistering mid-90 mph fastball and a low 80 mph change-up while keeping his arm motion virtually the same, making it extremely difficult for batters to read. His ability to change arm-angles was also effective at baffling his opponents.[179]

Over eighteen seasons, he compiled an impressive list of achievements. He was an eight-time All-Star (1996-2000, 2002, 2005-2006), three-time Cy Young winner (1997, 1998 and 2000), pitching Triple Crown winner (1999), All-Star Game MVP (1999) and World Series winner with the Red

---

179 James and Neyer, Op Cit.,.pp. 294-95.

Sox (2004). Martínez also led the American League in ERA five times (1997, 1999-2000, 2002-03) and was the strikeout leader three times (1999-2000, 2002). Overall, he compiled a 219-100 record (the second highest winning percentage in Major League history), 2.93 ERA, and 3,154 strike-outs. According to the stat much loved by sabermetricians, Martínez has the second best adjusted ERA of any pitcher in history.[180] I add to this list, not that any embellishment is required, a perfect inning.

Martínez's immaculate inning came on May 18th, 2002, at Fenway ver-sus the Mariners. While still early in the season, both clubs were off to a strong start: the Mariners were 29-13, Boston was 28-11.Though I have purposely stayed away from judging individual perfect innings, it is hard not to feel that opening a game by retiring the side on nine pitches makes the whole feat just a bit more exceptional. Facing the top of the order in Ichiro Suzuki, Mark McLemore, and Rubén Sierra, Martínez dismissed all three as follows: Suzuki was retired swinging, McLemore was caught looking and Sierra missed on strike three. Martínez pitched a total of 8 innings, allowing only 1 earned run off 6 hits. Having struck out 9 batters, Martínez received the win, with the final score, 4-1.

Prior to his immaculate inning, Martínez had a number of interesting brushes with perfection. The first was on April 13th, 1994. Playing in just his second start with the Montreal Expos, Martínez lost a perfect game with just a single out in the 8th by hitting Cincinnati Red's Reggie Sanders. While the result was a tussle on the mound, Sanders clearly upset by being hit by a pitch, it is difficult to accept that it was intentional given what was at stake in the game.[181] Martínez then gave up a single in the 9th, which ruined the chance for a no-hitter as well. He was removed after that so his near-perfect game was officially recorded as a no-decision. Again, on June 3[rd,] 1995, Martínez took a perfect game into the 9th with the Expos, retiring 27 Padres in a row. Scoreless through nine, the game went to extra innings; in the top of the 10th, Bip Roberts knocked a double to start the inning, forcing Felipe Alou to bring in Mel Rojas in relief of Martínez.[182]

---

180 "Career Leaders and Records for Adjusted ERA," Baseball Reference: http://www.baseball-reference.com/leaders/earned_run_avg_plus_career.shtml. Retrieved on December 2, 2014.

181 Norm King, "Pedro Martínez," SABR Bio Project. http://sabr.org/bioproj/person/a9ba2c91. Retrieved December on 2, 2014.

182 King, Op. cit.

He would come close one more time, this time as a Red Sox, taking a no-hitter into the 9th in a game against the Devil Rays on August 29th, 2000. Rays leadoff man, John Flaherty, was the spoiler.

In 2015, Pedro Martínez, along with Randy Johnson, John Smoltz and Craig Biggio were elected to the Hall of Fame.

Brian Lawrence
June 12th, 2002

Brian Michael Lawrence was the last of three pitchers to record an immaculate inning in the 2002 season. Born in Fort Collins, Colorado on May 14th, 1976, Lawrence was a seventeenth round draft pick of the San Diego Padres in the '98 draft. He made his debut appearance on April 15th, 2001, and played in San Diego for the next five seasons until he was traded in the off-season to the Washington Nationals. However, Lawrence never played for the Nationals after team doctors discovered an injury to his shoulder prior to the start of the '06 season. After being released by the Nationals, Lawrence signed with the Rockies, but was released again early in the 2007 season without making an appearance for them. The last team he played for was the New York Mets, making his final appearance in the Majors on September 17th, 2007.

A right-handed pitcher, the scouting report on Lawrence shows he relied mainly on his fastball and slider, though he also had a change-up that he used about 10-12% of the time.[183] Over his career, he posted a 50-63 record, with an ERA of 4.19, and 597 strikeouts.

On June 12th, 2002, Lawrence became the fiftieth Major Leaguer to pitch an immaculate inning. It occurred when the Padres took on the

---

183 "Brian Lawrence," FanGraphs: http://www.fangraphs.com/statss.aspx?playerid=1045 &position=P. Retrieved on November 18, 2014.

Orioles in an inter-league game at Camden Yards. Lawrence retired Brook Fordyce, Jerry Hairston Jr., and Melvin Mora on nine pitches in the bottom of the 3rd. All three batters struck out swinging. Lawrence stayed in the game until the top of the 9th, when he was replaced by Trevor Hoffman. Lawrence's Padres ended up winning, 2-0. He recorded the win, his seventh of the season, going 8 innings, allowing 5 hits, no runs, 1 walk and 7 strikeouts. Much later, Lawrence had this to say about his achievement: "It was awesome after the fact. I didn't know I did it at the time. I knew I struck out the side, but I didn't know I did it in nine pitches."[184]

In 2013, Lawrence became the pitching coach for the Lake Elsinore Storm in the California League.

184 Ryan Mersey, "Lawrence Relishing Coaching Opportunity," MILB.com (April 03, 2013): http://www.milb.com/news/article.jsp?ymd=20130304&content_id=42255814&fext=. jsp&vkey=news_t103&sid=t103

Brandon Backe
April 15th, 2004

No immaculate innings were recorded in the 2003 season, and it was almost two years before another pitcher, Brandon Backe, joined the elite club. Born on April 5th, 1978, in Galveston, Texas, Backe was drafted by the Tampa Bay Rays in the eighteenth round of the 1998 draft. He made his debut for the Rays on July 19th, 2002. Drafted as an infielder, and playing much of the minors in the outfield, Backe switched to pitching in 2001 and quickly rose through the Rays' minor league system. Backe ultimately spent two seasons with the Rays before being acquired by Houston. He played for the Astros from 2004 to 2009. Over his career, he recorded a 31-29 record, 5.23 ERA, and 360 strikeouts. A righted-handed pitcher, Backe's report indicates he had four main pitches: fastball, slider, curve and change-up. When he was with the Astros, he also threw a cutter on occasion. However, fastballs and sliders made up most his pitches (over 70%) over his eight-season career.[185]

On April 15th, 2004, Backe's Astros took on the Milwaukee Brewers. Backe entered the game in the 7th inning with the Astros already behind by 4 runs. After holding the Brewers scoreless, he again took the mound in the 8th to face Bill Hall, Scott Podsednik, and Craig Counsell. The trio were

---

185 "Brandon Backe," FanGraphs: http://www.fangraphs.com/statss.aspx?playerid=1529 &position=P. Retrieved on November 23, 2014.

retired on nine pitches: Hall and Podsednik went down looking, while Counsell struck out swinging. The Astros however, could not close the gap in the bottom of the frame and eventually lost, 6-2. For Backe, it was a strong performance, as he pitched 2 scoreless innings allowing no hits, no walks and striking out 4 batters.

Aside from his immaculate inning, Backe's off-field indiscretions placed him with a growing fraternity of players remembered more for what happened outside the diamond than on it. Backe and nine others were arrested by Galveston police on October 5th, 2008. Called to a wedding for a dispute involving an off-duty police officer in attendance working as a security guard, the police allegedly tasered someone and were involved in a violent scene. Charged with resisting arrest, Backe claimed his shoulder was significantly injured when he was pushed to the ground and beaten by officers.[186] Although Backe was not convicted, he and other guests who were injured that evening sued the Galveston Police Department. In the end, nine of the thirty officers who responded to the call were suspended and four received written reprimands. They were not held accountable for excessive force mind you, but for administrative violations regarding documentation of the events (failure to do paperwork in other words).[187] For Backe, the injury he received that evening ruined his career as a pitcher.[188] June 18th, 2009, was the last time Backe pitched in a Major League game.

186 Harvey Rice, "Ex-Astro says police ruined pitching career," *Houston Chronicle* (April 1, 2014): http://www.chron.com/neighborhood/bayarea/news/article/Ex-Astro-says-police-ruined-pitching-career-5368734.php. Retrieved on November 23, 2014.

187 "Police officers disciplined over wedding brawl," CNN.com (March 19, 2009): http://www.cnn.com/2009/CRIME/03/19/texas.wedding.brawl/. Retrieved on November 23, 2014.

188 David Brown, "Former Astros pitcher Brandon Backe alleges police brutality in civil trial," Yahoo, (April 02,2014): http://sports.yahoo.com/blogs/big-league-stew/former-astros-pitcher-brandon-backe-alleges-police-brutality-in-civil-trial-160806574.html. Retrieved on November 23, 2014.

Ben Sheets
June 13th, 2004

The second of three pitchers to record an immaculate inning in the 2004 season was Ben Sheets. Born on July 18th, 1978, in Baton Rouge, Louisiana, the right-handed starting pitcher played ten seasons in the Majors for the Milwaukee Brewers (2001-08), Oakland Athletics (2010) and Atlanta Braves (2012). Drafted tenth overall by the Brewers in the first round of the 1999 amateur draft, Sheets made his first appearance with Milwaukee on April 5th, 2001. Over his career, he mainly threw fastballs (63.1% of the time) and curves (30.1%), but also added in change-ups and sliders.[189] He finished professional baseball with a 94-96 record, 3.78 ERA, and 1,325 strikeouts. A four-time All-Star (2001, 2004, 2007, 2008), Sheets was also a member of the US Men's Olympic Baseball Team that captured gold at the 2000 Sydney Games.

On June 13th, 2004, Ben Sheets became the fifty-second pitcher in Major League history to record an immaculate inning. As is often the case, his perfect performance in a single inning did little to carry his club to victory. In a 5-4 loss to the Houston Astros at Miller Park, Sheets, the starting pitcher that day, took to the mound in the 3rd to face Pete Munro (batting 9th), Craig Biggio, and José Vizcaino. Sheets dismissed the side on

---

189 "Ben Sheets" FanGraphs: http://www.fangraphs.com/statss.aspx?playerid=710&position=P. Retrieved on December 2, 2014.

nine pitches, forcing all three hitters to strike out swinging. Sheets however, allowed another run in the top of the 6th, and finished the day having struck out 7 batters, while allowing 4 runs off 7 hits.

In 2004, Sheets' signed a $38.5 million four-year extension with the Brewers, which at the time was the largest contract in that club's history. Unfortunately, for the club and for Sheets, a series of troubling injuries sent him to the disabled list for long periods. Ailments included bulging discs in his spine, an inner ear infection that affected his balance, and shoulder tendonitis. In the 2008 off-season, after filing for free agency, Sheets had injury troubles again, this time having surgery to repair a torn flexor tendon in his elbow. It would be two more seasons before he played again for the Oakland A's. But once again, his season came to end thanks to the same injury to his elbow tendon. His final appearance was on October 3rd, 2012, with the Atlanta Braves. In July, 2014, Sheets was inducted into the Brewers Wall of Fame for pitching more than 1000 innings with the club.

LaTroy Hawkins
September 11th, 2004

Born on the winter solstice of 1972, LaTroy Hawkins was the final pitcher of the 2004 season to pitch a perfect inning. He has played in the Majors since 1995, making his first appearance with the Minnesota Twins on April 29th, 1995. To date, Hawkins has played with a total of ten different ball clubs during his tenure in the Majors: the Minnesota Twins (1995-2003), Chicago Cubs (2004-2005), San Francisco Giants (2005), Baltimore Orioles (2006), Colorado Rockies (2007, 2014), New York Yankees (2008), Houston Astros (2008-09), Brewers (2010-11), Angels (2012), and New York Mets (2013). A right-handed reliever, Hawkins is known for five pitches: a fastball in the mid-90s, a slider, a split-fingered fastball, a curve and change-up. Some sources have said he has a cut fastball, but not all agree.[190] According to FanGraphs, he has relied principally on his fastball (73.8% of the time) and slider (13.7%).[191] Drafted out of high school in the seventh round of the 1991 amateur draft by the Twins, by 2000 he had moved from the rotation to the bullpen where he has remained throughout his career. At the conclusion of the 2014 season, his career numbers include a 73-94 record, 4.33 ERA, 955 strikeouts and 125 saves.

---

190 James and Neyer, Op Cit. p.237.

191 "LaTroy Hawkins," FanGraphs: http://www.fangraphs.com/statss.aspx?playerid=729 &position=P. Retrieved on December 2, 2014.

On September 11ᵗʰ, 2004, Hawkins pitched an immaculate inning for the Chicago Cubs. Protecting a 3-run lead in the top of the 9ᵗʰ against the Florida Marlins, Hawkins needed just nine pitches to retire the side consisting of Jeff Conine, Juan Encarnación, and Alex González; all three of whom went out swinging. Hawkins was credited with the save. The Cubs won the game, 5 to 2.

At 41 years of age, it is remarkable Hawkins is still part of the show in 2015, especially given the many struggles he has had to endure over a long career. On September 27ᵗʰ, 2014, he made his 1000ᵗʰ career appearance in a game against the Dodgers, becoming just the sixteenth pitcher in MLB history to make 1000+ appearances. "A lot of good teammates, a lot of good mentors in the game. Plenty of blessings from the man upstairs to stay healthy", Hawkins said regarding this milestone. His prize that evening was a bottle of Dom Pérignon signed by his teammates.

Rick Helling
June 20th, 2006

Rick Allen Helling was a true all-around athlete over his career. Though he chose to play baseball, he was good enough to letter in football and basketball. Helling even played college football at Stanford University before being selected by the Texas Rangers in the first round of the '92 draft. Born on December 15th, 1970, Helling grew up in North Dakota, graduating from Bishop Shanley High School in Fargo. His first appearance with Texas occurred on April 10th, 1994. He spent a total of twelve seasons in the Majors, with five different clubs: the Rangers (1994-96 and 1997-2001), Marlins (1996-97 and 2003), Diamondbacks (2002), Orioles (2003) and Brewers (2005-06).

Helling played on the 2003 World Series winning Florida Marlins, having been traded from the Orioles earlier in the season. It was an interesting reversal of fortune, given that he was traded to the Rangers from the Marlins in 1997; the latter team would go on to win the World Series (though Helling did get a ring any way). His last appearance in the Majors was for the Milwaukee Brewers on September 9th, 2006. His career stats include a 93-81 record, 4.68 ERA and 1058 strikeouts. Unfortunately, he is also known to own records that most pitchers would not want on their résumé. In 2000, he became the first pitcher to give up 66 doubles in one season, breaking the previous record of 65 set back in 1970. Just one year later, he would better his own record, allowing 68 doubles in the '01 season. Also that year, he led the league in both home runs surrendered (38) and earned runs (124).

It was for activities off the field, however, that Helling may be forever remembered. This reputation came largely for the credit he received in Joe Torre and Tom Verducci's book *The Yankee Years*. Helling was identified as the whistleblower in what would become the biggest scandal in baseball since the 1919 Black Sox Affair. In the book, former Yankees pitcher David Cone singled-out Helling as having the "guts" to speak out about the use of performance enhancing drugs during the 1998 Executive Board Meeting of the Players Association. He told the group: "It's happening. It's real. And it's so prevalent that guys who aren't doing it are feeling pressure to do it because they're falling behind. It's not a level playing field. We've got to figure out a way to address it." [192] Baseball at the time was punch drunk giddy about exciting power hitters like Sammy Sosa, Ken Griffey Jr. and Mark McGwire. McGwire hit a record breaking seventy home runs that season and an estimated 43 million people tuned to watch him hit his 62nd homer that year.[193] The television numbers and general interest produced a collective sense of relief amongst owners and the League given that just four years previous the players and owners were locked in a season-ending labour dispute. Did anyone really care why these hitters were breaking records at such an astounding rate or that they were physically transforming right before our eyes? The answer seemed to be no. Despite Helling's warnings, it would not be until 2003 that Major League Baseball would start "survey testing" to estimate the extent of use of performance enhancing drugs among its players.

On June 20th, 2006, Helling became the fifty-fourth pitcher in the history of the Major Leagues to record an immaculate inning. Facing the top of the Detroit Tigers order in the 1st, he struck out Curtis Granderson, Placido Polanco and Ivan Rodriguez on just nine pitches. Both Granderson and Rodriguez were swinging strikeouts while Polanco was called out looking at the third pitch. Despite his immaculate performance that inning, Hellings' Brewers lost the game 10-1. Helling did not make it through the 2nd inning, giving up 6 hits and 7 runs, which is difficult to reconcile

192 Joe Torre and Tom Verducci, "The Man Who Warned Basball About Steriods," *Time* (Feb. 23, 2009): http://content.time.com/time/arts/article/0,8599,1881350,00.html. Retrieved on August 15, 2014.

193 Ibid

given his commanding performance in the 1st. Indeed, this is the perhaps the most egregious example of an immaculate inning not only being inconsequential to the ultimate outcome of the game, but the single worst follow-up inning to one that was so perfect.

Helling announced his retirement from Major League Baseball on February 5th, 2007, stating that he wanted to spend more time with his family: "I've said all along that I would retire if I couldn't do it anymore or if I couldn't be away from my family anymore. I couldn't handle being away from my family."[194] Given that he played on four different clubs from 2002 to 2006, it is little wonder he felt isolated from his family. In 2009, he became special assistant to Donald Fehr with the Players Association. A respected player who was not afraid to speak his mind, and armed with a degree in Economics from Stanford, Helling came to the job with good experience and credentials.

---

194 "Helling to retire after 12 seasons," ESPN.com: http://sports.espn.go.com/mlb/news/story?id=2755307. Retrieved on August 15, 2014.

Buddy Carlyle
July 6th, 2007

A number of notable events occurred during the 2007 Major League Baseball season. It was the sixtieth anniversary of Jackie Robinson's debut in the Majors, and players wore the number 42 on their jerseys to honor this historic event. Roy Halladay won his 100th game as a Toronto Blue Jay and Roger Clemens recorded his 350th career win with the Bronx Bombers. The Washington Nationals played their final game at Robert F. Kennedy stadium, while the Boston Red Sox won their second World Series in four years; a significant change for the once jinxed club. As far as immaculate innings go though, it was a comparatively slow season. Only one instance of the feat, by right-handed pitcher Buddy Carlyle, was recorded the whole season.

Born on December 21st, 1977, in Omaha, Nebraska, Carlyle was selected by the Cincinnati Reds during the second round of the 1996 draft. He made his debut in the Majors with the San Diego Padres on August 29th, 1999. Carlyle may be the textbook definition of a journeyman player, at least among the pitchers in this collection. He spent two seasons with the Padres before being sold to the Hanshin Tigers in the Nippon Professional Baseball League in Japan (2001-2002). He returned to the Majors in 2005, this time with the Los Angeles Dodgers. After another international stint in Korea, he returned to the Majors, playing for the Atlanta Braves (2007-09). Carlyle would again make his way to Japan to play a season with the

Hokkaido Nippon-Ham Fighters. He had a Major League appearance with the Yankees in 2011 and most recently (2014) was a call-up with the Mets. Over his career, Carlyle has relied mainly on his fastball (73.3% of the pitches he has thrown), but was known to throw a cutter (12.2%), curve (7.4%) and change-up (6.8%) also. On occasion, he also threw a slider, but only when he was with the Braves.[195] Through the end of the 2014 season, he had a 12-13 record, 5.12 ERA and 226 strikeouts. On July 6th, 2007, he pitched a perfect inning to add to his résumé.

It came in the 4th, with Carlyle pitching for the Brave's against his former club, the Padres. Working as a starting pitcher that day, Carlyle took the mound in the bottom half of the 4th to face Khalil Greene, Russell Branyan, and José Cruz Jr. Greene was called out swinging on the third pitch, a 94.7 mph fastball. Facing Branyan next, Carlyle got him with a high-fastball for strike three at 96.4 mph. Finally, Cruz was caught swinging and missing for the third and final out. Carlyle stayed in the game through to the end of the 8th, his club with a comfortable 4-run lead. Finishing as a 7-4 win for the Braves, Carlyle picked up the win, allowing only 3 runs off 8 hits, striking out 7 batters and walking 1 hitter.

At the time this was written, Carlyle was a free agent.

Buddy Carlyle's Perfect Inning Pitch by Pitch[196]

Batter	Pitch Count	Pitch Type	Speed	Strike
Khalil Greene	1	Fastball	92.5	Called Strike
	2	Curve	78.8	Called Strike
	3	Fastball	94.7	Swinging Strike
Russell Branyan	1	Change-up	81.9	Foul
	2	Change-up	85.0	Foul
	3	Fastball	96.4	Swinging Strike
José Cruz Jr.	1	Change-up	81.9	Called Strike
	2	Fastball	95.0	Swinging Strike
	3	Fastball	97.0	Swinging Strike

---

195 "Buddy Carlyle," FanGraphs: http://www.fangraphs.com/statss.aspx?playerid=2010& position=P. Retrieved on December 10, 2014.

196 Brooks Baseball Pitchf/x: http://www.brooksbaseball.net/pfxVB. Retrieved on November 11, 2014.

Rich Harden
June 8th, 2008

Richard ("Rich") Harden is the first, and only, Canadian-born pitcher to record an immaculate inning in the Majors. Born in Victoria, British Columbia on November 30th, 1981, the right-handed pitcher was drafted by the Seattle Mariners in the thirty-eighth round of the 1999 amateur draft. He opted to attend Central Arizona College instead and led the Division I Junior College League in 2001 with 127 strikeouts and a 2.14 ERA. He graduated that same year, and was drafted again in 2000 by the Oakland A's, this time in the seventeenth round. Harden made his first appearance in the Majors with the A's on July 21, 2003. Over his career, he played for the Athletics (2003-08, 2011), Cubs (2008-09) and Rangers (2010).[197] In 2011, he returned to Oakland on a one-year contract, but was traded to the Red Sox that July. A failed medical exam however, squashed the trade and Harden remained with Oakland for the rest of the season. In 2012, Harden did not play due to an injury and subsequent surgery to his shoulder. Following that season, Harden did not play in the Majors, and was released from a minor league contract with the Minnesota Twins in 2013.

Through the end of the 2011 season, Harden had a 59-38 record, 3.76 ERA, and 949 strikeouts. A right-handed pitcher, Harden utilized

---

197 "Rich Harden," Baseball Reference: http://www.baseball-reference.com/players/h/harderi01.shtml. Retrieved on December 10, 2014.

four pitches: a fastball, change-up, splitter and slider. The velocity on his fastball ranged from 92 to 96 mph. Harden's splitter has been called a "spuckle" (thanks to his catcher), because his grip makes it float a bit like a knuckleball.[198]

On June 8th, 2008, Harden made history in the 1st inning against the Angels with an immaculate inning. There is nothing quite as immaculate as retiring the side on nine pitches in the first inning, facing the top of the order. First up was Angels' shortstop, Maicer Izturis, who struck out with a foul tip into the glove of catcher Kurt Suzuki. Howie Kendrick swung through an 88.5 mph change-up for the second strike out. Anderson went down swinging on a change-up at 89 mph. The Oakland As won the game, 7-3, but it would take twelve innings to do it. Harden stayed in the game until the 6th, but left the game with his club trailing by 1 run. He finished the day having allowed just 2 runs off 7 hits. He also walked 3 batters, but managed to strike out 9 before being pulled. Brad Ziegler, not Harden, got the win that day. It took a total of 6 pitchers from the A's bullpen to finally win.

Rich Harden's Perfect Inning Pitch by Pitch[199]

Batter	Pitch Count	Pitch Type	Speed	Strike
	1	Fastball	92.0	Called Strike
Maicer Izturis	2	Change-up	86.9	Foul
	3	Fastball	97.0	Foul Tip
	1	Change-up	86.5	Foul
Howie Kendrick	2	Fastball	94.7	Swinging Strike
	3	Change-up	88.5	Swinging Strike
	1	Fastball	94.6	Swinging Strike
Garret Anderson	2	Fastball	96.0	Swinging Strike
	3	Change-up	89.0	Swinging Strike

198 http://www.baseballprospectus.com/article.php?articleid=12586. Retrieved on November 17, 2014.

199 Brooks Baseball Pitchf/x: http://www.brooksbaseball.net/pfxVB. Retrieved on November 11, 2014.

Félix Hernández
June 17th, 2008

The last pitcher to record a perfect inning in the 2008 season was none other than Félix Abraham (Garcia) Hernández. The "King", as he is called by Mariners fans, hails from Valencia, Venezuela and has played some truly remarkable baseball for most of his nine seasons in the Majors. Born on April 8th, 1986, Hernández was originally signed as a non-drafted free agent by the Mariners in 2002, shortly after he graduated from high school. It would be three more years before he made his Major League debut on August 4th, 2005, against the Tigers at the age of 19. In doing so, he became the youngest pitcher since José Rijo (who made his debut in 1984) to play in the Majors. Unlike many of the pitchers in the modern era, Hernández has played for the same team for his entire professional career—the Seattle Mariners.

Through to the end of the 2014 season, Hernández's numbers stack up this way: his win-loss record is 125-92, a 3.07 ERA and 1,974 strikeouts. A five-time All-Star (2009, 2011-2014), he led the American League in wins in 2009, won the 2010 Cy Young and was twice American League ERA leader in 2010 and 2014. He is also among the elite few in the game to have pitched a perfect game (versus Tampa Bay on August 15th, 2012).

A right-handed pitcher, he has a low to mid-90s fastball, as well as a curve, circle change-up and a slider.[200] Like many great pitchers, Hernández

---

200 "Félix Hernández," FanGraphs: http://www.fangraphs.com/statss.aspx?playerid=4772 &position=P. Retrieved on December 1, 2014.

relies on control as much as velocity. He can get great movement and sinking action on his pitches, particularly with his two-seam fastball. As a result, when he is on, he can induce a lot of groundballs and strikeouts.[201]

On June 17th, 2008, the Mariners took the field at Safeco to face the Florida Marlins. Hernández was the starting pitcher. After retiring the first three batters in order in the 1st, Hernández gave up a home run to Dan Uggla in the 2nd . The run scored closed the gap by one, with the Mariners having already put 2 runs on the board in the 1st. In the 4th, Hernández made history by retiring Jeremy Hermida (batting 2nd in the lineup), Jorge Cantú, and Mike Jacobs on nine pitches. The first two batters struck out swinging, while Jacobs was caught looking at strike three. The Mariners scored again in the 4th and the 5th, opening up a 4-run lead over the Marlins. Florida would have their revenge on Hernández in the 6th though: the first four batters would all single and a sacrifice fly from Cantú would bring the score to within 2 runs. In the 7th, Hernández again allowed one run closing the gap even further. His final appearance came in the 8th inning. Overall, he finished the day with a win (5 to 4), having pitched 7.2 innings, allowing 4 runs off 6 hits, walking 1 and striking out 9.

The King has his own court, a special section in Safeco Field in a foul territory section of the stands, near the left-field foul pole. On the days he pitches, you can follow his progress by the number of placards with large "K's", which are waved throughout the contest. If you choose to sit there, not only do you get a K-placard, but also a price discount on your ticket and a yellow t-shirt that reads, naturally, "King Félix."

---

201 Anthony Castrovince, "Craftier and wiser, Felix pitching better than ever," MLB.com (May 13, 2013): http://m.mariners.mlb.com/news/article/47399582/anthony-castrovince-craftier-and-wiser-felix-hernandez-pitching-better-than-ever. Retrieved on November 24, 2014.

A. J. Burnett
June 20th 2009

Have you ever wondered what A.J. stands for? Well, in the case of Major League pitcher A.J. Burnett, the answer is Allan James. Burnett was the first hurler in the 2009 season to pitch a perfect nine-pitch, three-out inning.

Burnett began his Major League career with the Florida Marlins, although he was first drafted by the Mets in the eighth round of the '95 amateur draft. He made his Major League debut on August 17th, 1999. Since then, he has played for the Marlins (1999-2005), Toronto Blue Jays (2006-08), New York Yankees (2009-11), Pirates (2012-2013, 2015), and Phillies (2014).

Burnett has four pitches: fastball (four-seam), slider, curve and change-up. Over his career, he has relied mainly on his fastball (64.1%), curve (29.5%), and occasionally, his change-up (6.2%).[202] Although his velocity has declined somewhat since 2007, his main career struggles have been with control. Burnett has twice led the Majors in wild pitches and hit batters. Despite these control problems, he also led the American League in strikeouts in 2008 with 231, and the National League with five shutouts in 2002. To add to these accomplishments, he also notched a no-hitter against the San Diego Padres on May 12th, 2001 (although he did allow

202 "A.J. Burnett," FanGraphs: http://www.fangraphs.com/statss.aspx?playerid=512&position=P. Retrieved on December 10, 2014.

9 walks). Burnett was also the first Yankee in team history to record four consecutive strikeouts in one inning, and in 2013, he became the first right-handed pitcher in Pirates history to record more than 200 strikeouts in a single season. Burnett has played on two World Series teams, first with the Marlins in 2002 and then with the Yankees in 2009. Through the end of the 2014, he had a career win-loss record of 155-150, 4.04 ERA, and 2,370 strikeouts. He also had a perfect inning on June 20th, 2009.

His immaculate inning came in the 3rd inning of a game against his former club, the Marlins. The Marlins opened the scoring that day with a solo home run shot in the 2nd by Dan Uggla. In the top of the 3rd, Burnett faced Josh Johnson, Chris Coghlan, and Emilio Bonifacio. All three batters were struck out swinging. Burnett remained in the game until the 7th inning. With his club behind by 1 run, Joe Girardi allowed his pitcher to face two hitters, one of whom got a single, before ending his day. The Yankees offence could not produce the single run needed to force extra innings, and the Marlins won the game, 2-1. For Burnett, his numbers over 6.2 innings looked like this: 2 runs off 5 hits, 3 bases on balls and 8 strikeouts on the day.

After just one season with the Phillies in 2014, Burnett signed a one-year, $8.5 million contract to return to his former club, the Pittsburgh Pirates. The 2014 season was not an easy one for A.J. Diagnosed with an inguinal hernia, he struggled that season with an 8-18 record, 4.59 ERA and took top honours in the league for most walks at 96. Given that he signed for more than $4 million less than what he was offered by the Phillies, it is clear he is banking on a reversal of fortunes on the field with his old team (I am sure pitching for a contending club also influenced his decision).

Ross Ohlendorf
September 5th, 2009

The second and final immaculate inning pitched in the 2009 season came from Pirate Ross Ohlendorf on September 5th. Born in Austin, Texas on August 8th, 1982, Curtis Ross Ohlendorf is the son of a Texas rancher and continues to this day to help run the family business, known as the Texas Longhorn Ranch. In high school, he played both basketball and baseball for St. Stephens Episcopal School, graduating in 2001. An academic student and an athlete, Ohlendorf attended Princeton, where he majored in Operations Research and Financial Engineering. His undergraduate thesis examined the financial success of Rule IV Drafts in Major League Baseball from 1989 to 1993. While there, he pitched for the Tigers (Princeton's team), and was named rookie of the year in 2002. Drafted in 2004 by the Arizona Diamondbacks in the fourth round, it would be another two years until Ohlendorf finally graduated from Princeton. His academic success mixed with his athletic pursuits certainly did not go unnoticed. He was awarded the George Meuller Award from Princeton, in recognition of his ability to succeed both academically and in athletics. In 2010, the *Sporting News* named him as number three in the top twenty smartest athletes in sports.

Ohlendorf made his Major League debut with the New York Yankees on September 11th, 2007. A righted-handed starting pitcher, the scouting report on Ross describes him as "large-framed" with a "low three-quarter arm slot." He has an 89-92 mph fastball that has some sink and an

80-85 mph "decent" slider and "good change-up".[203] He played for four Major League clubs between 2007 and 2013: the Yankees (2007-08), Pirates (2008-2011) Padres (2012), and the Nationals (2013). Through the end of 2013, he recorded a 22-33 record, 4.88 ERA and 357 strikeouts.

On September 5th, 2009, Ohlendorf added pitching an immaculate inning to his career achievements. Facing Khalil Greene, Julio Lugo, and Jason LaRue from the St. Louis Cardinals in the top of the 7th, he retired all three batters on nine pitches. To Greene, he pitched three sliders all in the high 70s to low 80s. Next up, Lugo swung through strike three while LaRue fanned on a slider for strike three. Ohlendorf pitched eight innings, allowing only 4 hits and 1 run that day—though the Pirates lost to the Cardinals, 2-1. After the game, Ohlendorf had this to say about his perfect inning: "That's pretty cool. It actually crossed my mind after about the fifth pitch because I don't think I've ever done that. Ryan (Doumit; the catcher) did a great job. I threw a lot of sliders that bounced tonight, and he did a great job of knocking them down."[204]

Before moving on to our next pitcher, I felt it was worthwhile returning to Ohlendorf's academic work, as he is the only pitcher in this collection to have produced a thesis as part of his undergraduate education. It involved the use of sabermetrics to determine the value of players drafted between 1989 and 1993. Specifically, he used Bill James' win-shares formula to determine the value of each player, and whether the signing bonuses offered to players were worth the initial investment. While many of the players in the draft did make the Majors, those who did, tended to produce high rates of return on investment for their clubs, about 60% in fact. According to Ohlendorf, the data show that "if you invest $1, it will grow to $1.60 after a year and $2.56 after two years, and so on ... I believe the stock market has had a historical rate of about 7% or 8% prior to the last year. So even though many of the investments did not work out ... signing the high picks to large bonuses appears to have been a very smart investment."[205] During

---

203 "Ross Ohlendorf," Sox Prospects: http://www.soxprospects.com/players/ohlendorf-ross.htm. Retrieved on October 3, 2014.

204 Dejan Kovacevic, "Ohlendorf's historic inning wasted in Pirates' 2-1 loss," *Pittsburgh Post-Gazette*, (September 6, 2009): http://www.post-gazette.com/sports/pirates/2009/09/06/Ohlendorf-s-historic-inning-wasted-in-Pirates-2-1-loss/stories/200909060161. Retrieved on October 30, 2014.

205 Tim Kurkjian, "Ohlendorf brimming with intelligence," ESPN.com (June 6, 2009): http://sports.espn.go.com/mlb/columns/story?columnist=kurkjian_tim&id=4230662. Retrieved on October 31, 2014.

that period, the average signing bonus was $210,235, whereas the average rate of return was $2,468,127. His is an interesting example of a ballplayer using sabermetrics for a practical purpose.

At the end of the 2014 season, a season plagued by injuries, Ohlendorf became a free agent, having been out-righted off the 40-man roster of the Washington Nationals.

Ross Ohlendorf's Perfect Inning Pitch by Pitch[206]

Batter	Pitch Count	Pitch Type	Speed	Strike
	1	Slider	78.8	Called Strike
Khalil Greene	2	Slider	81.7	Swinging Strike
	3	Slider	82.6	Swinging Strike
	1	Fastball	93.0	Called Strike
Julio Lugo	2	Slider	82.2	Called Strike
	3	Slider	82.4	Swinging Strike
	1	Slider	81.2	Called Strike
Jason LaRue	2	Slider	82.1	Swinging Strike
	3	Slider	83.9	Swinging Strike

206 Brooks Baseball Pitchf/x: http://www.brooksbaseball.net/pfxVB. Retrieved on October 31, 2014.

Rafael Soriano
August 23rd, 2010

Almost a year after Ross Ohlendorf's immaculate accomplishment, Dominican-born reliever Rafael Soriano became the sixtieth pitcher in baseball history to pitch a perfect inning. Born on December 19th, 1979, in San Jose, San Pedro de Macoris in the Dominican Republic, Soriano made his Major League debut with the Seattle Mariners on May 10th, 2002. Over his career, he has played for five clubs: the Mariners (2002-06), Braves (2007-09), Rays (2010), Yankees (2011-12) and Nationals (2013-14). At the end of the 2014 season, Soriano has a career 22-28 record, 2.85 ERA, 637 strikeouts, and 207 saves. An All-Star in 2010, Soriano led the American League in saves in 2010 and was named the American League Rolaids Relief Man Award that same year.

According to FanGraphs, Soriano mostly relies on his fastball (60.9% of the pitches he has thrown over his career), a four-seam pitch that typically clocks in the low to mid-90s. He also uses a slider about 24% of the time, and a cutter, which over his career he has used about 12.5% of the time.[207]

Soriano's immaculate inning occurred on the August 23rd, 2010, in game against the Angels. Soriano made his appearance in the bottom of the 9th as the closer. Called on to protect a slim 1-run lead, he took the

---

207 "Rafael Soriano," FanGraphs: http://www.fangraphs.com/statss.aspx?playerid=1100 &position=P. Retrieved on December 12, 2014.

mound to face the bottom of the order. Unlike many of his contemporaries in this collection, Soriano offered up a steady diet of fastballs to retire the side on nine pitches. First was Erick Aybar, who struck out on a 96.2 mph scorcher that was foul tipped into the glove of Kelly Shoppach. Next up was pinch-hitter Mike Napoli, who swung on and missed for strike three. Finally, Peter Bourjous received 3 fastballs, from 94 to 95 mph. Like Napoli, Bourjous was able to foul-off the second pitch, but the other two offerings were clean strikes. With that, Soriano received the save and the Rays won 4-3. For those paying close attention, Soriano is one of only six pitchers to have recorded immaculate inning that also resulted in a save.

Soriano has had more than his fair share of injuries as a professional pitcher. A torn ulnar collateral ligament, sustained during his time in Triple-A in the Pacific Coast League, led to Tommy John surgery in 2004. In August, 2006, he was struck behind the ear by a line drive off Angels' power hitter Vladimir Guerrero, resulting in a concussion. He has not played a game in the Majors since September 26th, 2014.

Rafael Soriano's Perfect Inning Pitch by Pitch[208]

Batter	Pitch Count	Pitch Type	Speed	Strike
	1	Fastball	93.7	Called Strike
Erick Aybar	2	Fastball	94.2	Swinging Strike
	3	Fastball	96.2	Foul Tip
	1	Fastball	96.4	Swinging Strike
Mike Napoli	2	Fastball	95.4	Foul
	3	Fastball	92.3	Swinging Strike
	1	Fastball	94.5	Called Strike
Peter Bourjous	2	Fastball	94.7	Foul
	3	Fastball	93.8	Swinging Strike

208 Brooks Baseball Pitchf/x: http://www.brooksbaseball.net/pfxVB. Retrieved on December 11, 2014.

Jordan Zimmermann
May 6th, 2011

The first of two immaculate innings in the 2011 season came by way of Jordan Zimmermann, a right-handed starting pitcher for the Washington Nationals. Drafted in the second round of the 2007 draft, Zimmermann made his debut with that club on April 20th, 2009. According to the scouting reports, he is known for three pitches: a four-seam fastball (which tops out at 98 mph), a slider and a curveball. Zimmermann refers to his slider as a "baby cutter" because it does not have quite the same movement that other pitchers have. His curveball is typically between 78 and 80 mph.[209] Twice an All-Star in 2013 and 2014, Zimmermann was also a co-leader in wins for the National League in 2013. Through the end of the 2014 season, he had a career record of 57-40, 3.24 ERA, and 739 strikeouts. To date, he has played his entire career with the Nationals.

On May 6th, 2011, the visiting Washington Nationals took on the Marlins in Miami. In the bottom of the 2nd inning, facing the middle of the order in Giancarlo Stanton, Greg Dobbs, and John Buck, Zimmermann's performance was immaculate. Retiring all three on nine pitches, Stanton and Dobbs went out swinging, while John Buck was caught looking.

---

209 David Laurila, "Q&A with Jordan Zimmermann," FanGraphs (June 13, 2012): http://www.fangraphs.com/blogs/qa-jordan-zimmermann-gio-gonzalez/. Retrieved on December 12, 2014.

Zimmerman however, went on to allow 2 runs off 5 hits, and 2 walks over 6 innings. His teammate Drew Storen recorded the win, with the help of closer Sean Burnett who got a save for his efforts. The Nationals won, 3-2.

In 2013, Zimmermann set another career record by pitching his first career shutout against the Reds. Allowing only one hit, Zimmerman's performance came on the heels of a one-hit, one-run game pitched by teammate Gio Gonzalez the previous night. Washington fans would have to look back to 1917 to find another instance when the team produced back-to-back one-hit games. The pitchers then were Walter Johnson and Doc Ayers, who held the White Sox to just two hits in two games. Zimmerman remarked "I'm just throwing strikes and trying to get ahead of guys and not trying to get deep in the counts and letting them put the ball in play."[210] In 2014, late in September on the last day of the season, Zimmermann again made the record books, throwing a no-hitter against the Florida Marlins. It was the first no-hitter in Nationals' history (but the fifth if you include the years the club was located in Montreal).[211]

---

210 James Wagner, "Jordan Zimmermann and Nationals one-hit Reds for second night in a row," *Washington Post* (April 26, 2013): http://www.washingtonpost.com/sports/nationals/jordan-zimmermann-and-nationals-one-hit-reds-for-second-night-in-a-row/2013/04/26/5e05b3d2-aed8-11e2-a986-eec837b1888b_story.html. Retrieved on December 10, 2014.

211 Ted Berg, "Nationals outfielder makes miraculous catch to save Jordan Zimmermann's no-hitter," *USA Today* (September 28, 2014): http://ftw.usatoday.com/2014/09/nationals-outfielder-makes-miraculous-catch-to-save-jordan-zimmermanns-no-hitter. Retrieved on December 10, 2014.

Juan Peréz
July 8th, 2011

Sloppy Thurston and Juan Peréz hold the extremely rare distinction of being the only two immaculate inning pitchers to hurl their nine-pitch, three-strikeout, effort during extra innings. Peréz was the second and final pitcher to record a perfect inning in 2011. Born in Villa Riva, Dominican Republic, Peréz made his Major League debut for the Pirates on September 7th, 2006. Originally signed as an amateur free agent by the Red Sox in 1998, Peréz has played for four clubs in the Majors: the Pirates (2006-2007), Phillies (2011), Brewers (2012) and Blue Jays (2013).

A left-handed pitcher, Peréz has relied mainly on his fastball (low 90s) and slider (low 80s), although he sometimes throws a change-up. With the '07 Pirates, he threw a curve ball (high 70s) a little less than a third of the time.[212] Through the 2013 season, Peréz had a 2-4 record, 4.25 ERA and 64 strikeouts.

It was with the Phillies that Peréz achieved his perfect inning. On July 8th, 2011, the Phillies (55-33 at the time) squared off against the Braves (53-36) in an extra innings contest at Citizens Bank Park. The starting pitchers that day were Roy Halladay for the Phillies and Brandon Beachy for the Braves. However, before the end of the game, both teams would send a total of ten pitchers to the mound. In the top of the 10th in a tied game,

---

212 "Juan Peréz," FanGraphs: http://www.fangraphs.com/statss.aspx?playerid=2557& position=P. Retrieved on November 16, 2014.

Juan Peréz faced the bottom of the Braves order. First up, Jason Heyward, looked at two sliders for strikes before swinging at strike three. Next up, Nate McLouth faced a 94 mph fastball and 84 mph slider for the first two strikes before he struck out swinging on a slider. Wilkin Ramírez received a fastball-slider-fastball combination and was retired swinging on a high, inside pitch. It proved to be the final inning of the game, as Raul Ibañez hit a solo home run shot in the bottom of the 10th to end the game, 3-2. Juan Peréz recorded the win. Speaking in his native Spanish, Juan had this to say after his outing: "I got a lot of faith in God, and I thought that if I stayed in the game at some point, it's gonna happen."[213] The last Phillies pitcher to record an immaculate inning before Peréz was Andy Ashby in 1991.

Juan Peréz played his final game in the Majors on August 10th, 2013. The Blue Jays moved him to the 60-day disabled list, resulting from a partially torn ulnar collateral ligament. Peréz opted for rehab over surgery to repair the ligament. Manager John Gibbons remarked: "Juan's not a young guy. He's a warrior. He's a great competitor. He's done a great job for us. It's unfortunate. We don't know how it's going to end up.[214] He was released by the Jays in March, 2014, but signed with the Braves six days later.

Juan Peréz's Perfect Inning Pitch by Pitch[215]

Batter	Pitch Count	Pitch Type	Speed	Strike
Jason Heyward	1	Slider	81.2	Called Strike
	2	Slider	82.7	Called Strike
	3	Slider	84.5	Swinging Strike
Nate McLouth	1	Fastball	94.7	Called Strike
	2	Slider	84.3	Called Strike
	3	Slider	83.0	Swinging Strike (Blocked)
Wilkin Ramírez	1	Fastball	95.2	Called Strike
	2	Slider	83.8	Swinging Strike
	3	Fastball	95.3	Swinging Strike

213 Nate Mink, "Perez strikes out side on nine pitches," MLB.com (July 9, 2011): http://m. phillies.mlb.com/news/article/21631308/. Retrieved on November 18, 2014.

214 John Lott, "Blue Jays' Juan Perez lands on 60-day DL with torn elbow ligament," *National Post* (Aug. 10, 2013): http://sports.nationalpost.com/2013/08/10/blue-jays-juan-perez-lands-on-60-day-dl-with-torn-elbow-ligament/.

215 Brooks Baseball Pitchf/x: http://www.brooksbaseball.net/pfxVB. Retrieved on November 16, 2014.

Clay Buchholz
August 16th, 2012

Red Sox pitcher Clay Buchholz was the sixty-third pitcher to post an immaculate inning in professional baseball. Buchholz has pitched with the Red Sox organization since 2007. Other than his immaculate inning, he made the record books in just his second start (September 1st, 2007), recording a no-hitter against the Orioles. He was only the third player on his first or second start to ever accomplish this in Major League Baseball. He was the first Red Sox rookie pitcher to throw a no-hitter, and the seventeenth overall in franchise history. Not a bad start indeed. It was later learned that manager Terry Francona and general manager Theo Epstein were both concerned about Buchholz, and had spoken during that game about his high pitch count. They decided to set the total at 120, a high total given he had never thrown more than 98 pitches in a game all season. In fact, Buchholz finished the game on 115 pitchers, suggesting Francona was more than a bit reluctant to remove his young pitcher on the verge of making history. Through the end of the 2014 season, Buchholz has a career win-loss record of 66-44, 3.92 ERA, and 699 strikeouts. A two-time All-Star (2010, 2013), he was also part of the World Series Boston Red Sox team in 2013.

On August 16th, 2012, Buchholz pitched his immaculate inning against the division rival Orioles at Camden Yards. While Buchholz had begun the 2012 season with an impressive 8-2 record, his placement on the 15-day disabled list foreshadowed a future diagnosis of esophagitis, a serious inflammation of the esophagus. However, there was no sign of trouble in mid-August. Protecting a 3-run lead, Buchholz began the 6th inning facing Adam Jones, Matt Wieters and Chris Davis. Jones was in a contract year and playing for the best deal he could get with an average over .300 and 14 home runs and 33 RBIs in the first 46 games of the season. Facing Buchholz, Jones watched strike three fly past him, right at the knees. Next up, Matt Wieters also struck out looking. With two down on six pitches, Chris Davis stepped into the batter's box and after fouling two off the first base side, chased the third pitch for the final out. The immaculate 6th completed, Buchholz stayed in the game until the end of the 8th. The Red Sox would take the game. Afterwards manager Bobby Valentine, a hated man by Red Sox fans that year, described Buchholz as a man possessed.[216]

Buchholz finished the 2012 season with an 11-8 record and a 4.56 ERA. Not his best year or his worst. As with many of the immaculate innings, while it was a personal triumph for the pitcher, overall, the good fortune of that night did little for a Red Sox team that was struggling. The team finished their 2012 season, the centenary of Fenway Park, with a 69-93 record and a last place finish in the American League East. Overall, they were the third worst team in the AL. On the final day of the season, Red Sox management fired Bobby Valentine after only one, very tumultuous, season. Nobody, least of all Valentine, was surprised.

More recently, Buchholz has again been in the spotlight, but not for pitching excellence. In May, 2013, former pitching great Jack Morris accused Buchholz of throwing a spitball. According to Morris: "What do you think? Look at the pitches. Fastball at 94 that goes like that. On a fastball? He's not the first guy to ever do it. You can get away with it. Gaylord [Perry] made a nice career out of it."[217] The controversy was fuelled by Buchholz's wet hair and the appearance of what one former MLB Now analyst described as a "white-substance" on his hair and

---

216 Kevin Kaduk, "Clay Buchholz throws 'immaculate' inning, strikes out three Orioles with nine pitches,". Big League Stew (Aug 17, 2012): http://sports.yahoo.com/blogs/mlb-big-league-stew/clay-buchholz-throws-immaculate-inning-strikes-three-orioles-144938772--mlb.html. Retrieved on August 1, 2013.

217 David Schoenfield, "Is Buchholz cheating? Jack Morris thinks so," ESPN.com (May 03, 2013): http://espn.go.com/blog/sweetspot/post/_/id/35449/is-buchholz-cheating-jack-morris-thinks-so. Retrieved on August 2, 2013.

fingers.[218] Not surprisingly, Buchholz responded to the accusations by shaking them off: "I laughed at it that day. I laughed at it as soon as they started talking about it. I know it's been the talk all week, but I'm fine with it. It is what it is."[219] Time may have proven his accusers wrong. At the very least, talk of Buchholz alleged cheating faded from the news pretty quickly.

Clay Buchholz's Perfect Inning Pitch by Pitch[220]

Batter	Pitch Count	Pitch Type	Speed	Strike
	1	Curve	78	Called Strike
Adam Jones	2	Curve	78.6	Called Strike
	3	Cutter	91.3	Called Strike
	1	Sinker	92.5	Foul
Matt Wieters	2	Cutter	90.3	Swinging Strike
	3	Sinker	94.5	Called Strike
	1	Fastball	93.3	Foul
Chris Davis	2	Cutter	91.9	Foul
	3	Splitter	87.6	Swinging Strike

218 Nick Cafardo, "Red Sox pitcher Clay Buchholz accused of cheating" *Boston Globe* (May 03, 2013): http://www.bostonglobe.com/sports/2013/05/02/red-sox-pitcher-clay-buchholz-accused-cheating/DKyrT0dn8EQmW4idbut8YI/story.html. Retrieved on August 2, 2013.

219 John Tomase, "Cheating non-troversy: Clay Buchholz to maintain routine," *Boston Herald* (May 06, 2013): http://bostonherald.com/sports/red_sox_mlb/boston_red_sox/2013/05/cheating_non_troversy_clay_buchholz_to_maintain_routine. Retrieved on August 2, 2013.

220 Brooks Baseball Pitchf/x: http://www.brooksbaseball.net/pfxVB. Retrieved on November 15, 2014.

Wade Miley
October 1st, 2012

The last immaculate inning pitched in 2012 was by left-hander Wade Miley. Born on November 13th, 1986, in Hammond, Louisiana, Miley's scouting report shows he is a four-pitch hurler: four-seam and two-seam fastballs (typically ranging from the high 80s to the low 90s), a slider and a change-up.[221] He also has a curve (low 70s) he uses sometimes, especially with right-handers. Drafted by the Diamondbacks forty-third overall in the first round of the 2008 amateur draft, Miley played his first game for Arizona on August 20th, 2011 at the age of 24. Through 2014, he has only played for the Diamondback organization. An All-Star in 2012, Miley was also was named National League Rookie of the Month for April, going 3-0, with a 1.29 ERA, and 15 strikeouts over 21 innings. He has a career win-loss record of 38-35, 3.79 ERA, and 499 strikeouts. On April 22nd, 2013, Miley also recorded his first, and so far only, home run.

On October 1st, 2012, the Rockies took on the Diamondbacks at Chase Field in an over four-hour long evening game. In a pitching marathon of epic proportions, the Rockies and Diamondbacks sent a total of fifteen pitchers to the mound in a contest that lasted 13 innings before

---

221 "Wade Miley Player Card," Brooks Baseball: http://www.brooksbaseball.net/landing.php?player=489119. Retrieved on November 15, 2014.

Colorado emerged as 7-5 winners. In the top of the 3rd, starter Wade Miley faced the 8th, 9th and 1st batters in the Colorado line-up, protecting a slim 1-run lead. First up, Herrera received three fastballs, all in the low 90s, and struck out swinging on a high and inside fastball just under 92 mph. Next up, Drew Pomeranz swung through a slider for strike three, quickly followed by Josh Rutledge swinging through a 92 mph fastball for strike three. Miley made it to the 8th before finally being replaced by David Hernandez after giving up back-to-back run-scoring doubles to Rutledge and Colvin. Having blown a 2-1 lead, it was up to the bullpen to hold off the Rockies and allow the offense back into the game. After a solo homer in the bottom of the 9th by Goldschmidt tied the game and sent it into extras, the Rockies eventually scored 4 runs in the 13th and took the game. Overall, Miley pitched 7.2 innings, allowing 3 earned runs off 6 hits, while striking out 10 batters.

It is not too surprising that Miley pitched a perfect inning in 2012, given the remarkable rookie season he was having. The game in question was his last of the season; however, much of the game commentary focused less on Miley's immaculate inning and more on his determination in a game his team ultimately lost. With a disappointing season winding down, the commentary also discussed what went wrong over the year and what needed to be fixed. Only the writers took the time to notice the perfect inning in the 3rd and acknowledged that only two pitchers DBacks other ever achieved such a feat.[222] Reflecting on his 2012 season, Miley had this to say: "I had a decent year. Still got a lot of things to work on. Just going to sharpen up everything I can."[223]

222 Tyler Emerick, "Miley strikes out 10, but D-backs fall in 13," MLB.com (Oct. 02, 2012): http://arizona.diamondbacks.mlb.com/mlb/gameday/index.jsp?gid=2012_10_01_colmlb_arimlb_1&mode=recap&c_id=ari. Retrieved on November 15, 2014.

223 Sarah McLellan, "Arizona Diamondbacks' Wade Miley displays determination," AZCentral Sports (Oct. 2, 2012): http://www.azcentral.com/sports/diamondbacks/articles/2012/10/02/20121002arizona-diamondbacks-wade-miley-displays-determination.html. Retrieved November 15th, 2014.

Wade Miley's Perfect Inning Pitch by Pitch[224]

Batter	Pitch Count	Pitch Type	Speed	Strike
Johnathan Herrera	1	Fastball	92.0	Called Strike
	2	Fastball	92.2	Fouled
	3	Fastball	91.8	Swinging Strike
Drew Pomeranz	1	Fastball	93.3	Called Strike
	2	Fastball	93.3	Swinging Strike
	3	Slider	83.0	Swinging Strike
Josh Rutledge	1	Fastball	93.7	Called Strike
	2	Fastball	93.4	Fouled
	3	Fastball	92.7	Swinging Strike

---

224 Brooks Baseball Pitchf/x: http://www.brooksbaseball.net/pfxVB. Retrieved on November 15, 2014.

Iván Nova
May 29th, 2013

Born on January 12th, 1987, in Palenque, San Cristobal, Dominican Republic, Iván Nova is a right-handed pitcher for the New York Yankees and the sixty-fifth pitcher to record an immaculate inning. The Yankees signed the young pitcher as an international free agent in 2004. It would be four more years until Nova was added to the 40-man roster, and two more seasons before he made his debut in the Majors (May 13th, 2010). Nova has four pitches and great velocity: a four-seam fastball (91 to 95 mph), a slider/cutter fastball (85 to 89 mph), a change-up (85 to 88 mph) and curve (79 to 81 mph). Through to the end of 2014, Nova's career numbers include a 40-22 record, 4.20 ERA, and 405 strikeouts.

Nova's immaculate performance came against the cross-town rival Mets at Yankee Stadium on May 29th, 2013. By the top of the 5th inning, when Nova came in to relieve Adam Warren, the Yankees were already behind, 8-1. Still in the game in the top of the 8th, Nova faced the 8th, 9th and 1st batters. First up, Ike Davis, got three straight curves for strikes. Next, Mike Baxter, looked at strike one, fouled off a 96 mph sinker and then swung on a curve ball for strike three. Nova then retired Rubén Tejada on a fastball-cutter-curve combination, with Tejada swinging on the third pitch. Both teams eventually added more runs to their totals but the gap remained the same: the Mets took the contest 9-4. Nova's numbers for the day were nothing to be ashamed about: he pitched 5 innings and allowed only 1 earned run on 5 hits, giving up 1 walk and striking out 6 batters. After the game, the young pitcher said his performance "was a good one; I was feeling really well, throwing a lot of strikes and I was aggressive. I went after hitters and I had good stuff today, so it's a good one."[225]

More recently, Nova experienced a tough 2014. He was unable to complete his April 19th start due to pain in his right elbow. He was diagnosed with a partially torn ulnar collateral ligament that required Tommy John surgery and sat out the rest of the season. The pain in his elbow may have been the cause of what was otherwise a disappointing beginning to the season: in just four starts, he had an ERA of 8.27, and 1.84 WHIP.

Iván Nova's Perfect Inning Pitch by Pitch[226]

Batter	Pitch Count	Pitch Type	Speed	Strike
	1	Curve	82.3	Swinging Strike
Ike Davis	2	Curve	82.6	Called Strike
	3	Curve	84.1	Swinging Strike
	1	Curve	82.3	Called Strike
Mike Baxter	2	Sinker	96.0	Fouled
	3	Curve	84.2	Swinging Strike
	1	Fastball	96.8	Fouled
Rubén Tejada	2	Cutter	96.6	Fouled
	3	Curve	84.0	Swinging Strike

225 Josh Vitale, "Nova makes history with 3 K's on nine pitches," MLB.com (May 29, 2013): http://m.mlb.com/news/article/49014250/yankees-right-hander-ivan-nova-makes-history-with-three-strikeouts-on-nine-pitches. Retrieved on November 16, 2014.

226 Brooks Baseball Pitchf/x: http://www.brooksbaseball.net/pfxVB. Retrieved on November 14th, 2014.

Steve Delabar
July 30th, 2013

The next immaculate inning came at the hand of Toronto Blue Jays reliever, Steve Delabar. While the Jays were having a remarkably bad 2013, especially given the expectations coming into the season, Delabar was having the best year of his professional career. It only seems fitting that a pitcher, who was in the midst of the most improbable of comebacks, would cap it off with a most improbable feat.

Flash back to 2011, Delabar was 28, working as a substitute high-school teacher and finishing his degree at a local university. Clearly, he was planning on another career outside professional baseball. Then something quite unexpected happened.

The twenty-ninth pick overall for the San Diego Padres in 2003, Delabar's career seemed to have come to an unfortunate end.[227] While pitching for the Brockton Rox in the Can-Am League, Delabar suffered a fracture to his right elbow. The injury, coupled with the fact he had never played above Class A ball, made the prospect of a comeback very unlikely. Working as a coach at his old instructors place in Kentucky in 2011, Delebar began to use a weighted ball training program, less for his own benefit and more to pass the experience on to his students. Delabar

227 Gregor Chisholm, "All-Star Game would be Delabar's Hollywood ending," MLB.com (July 11, 2013)

and his former instructor were amazed as his pitching kept improving to a point where his dreams of playing in the big leagues seemed much less like a pipe dream, and more like a real possibility.

Astonishingly, after a couple of bullpen sessions for the Mariners, Delabar was signed. He made his Major League debut as a September call-up in 2011. On September 15th, 2011, he recorded his first win against the Yankees. In July, 2012, he was traded to the Blue Jays for outfielder Eric Thames.

In the '12-'13 off-season, Jays General Manager, Alex Anthopoulos, made a series of impressive trades that got the attention of professional baseball and ignited the imagination of championship-starved Toronto fans. It had been twenty years since the Jays had won the World Series and the drought in the ensuing years were harsh, as the team had not had even a sniff of post-season play since the highly successful teams of the early '90s. Anthopoulos acquired a who's who of pitching excellence, including the 2012 Cy Young winning knuckleballer, R.A. Dickey, from the Mets to go with Josh Johnson and Mark Buehrle from the Marlins. In a short time, the Jays had a powerhouse starting rotation, at least on paper, making them a serious contender for top spot in the super-competitive American League East. However, 2013 ultimately saw the starters fail to live up to expectations. Instead, it was the bullpen that garnered all the accolades. In the first half of the season, Brett Cecil and Steve Delabar where among the only bright lights on a team that struggled. By mid-season, Delabar had posted an impressive 5-1 record, 1.74 ERA and 54 strikeouts. Suddenly, the minor league pitcher who typically threw between 89 and 91 mph, was gaining a reputation as a hard-throwing righty. In July, he was named as the final player to the American League All-Star Team; the result of a campaign that netted him 9.6 million votes from exuberant Toronto fans.[228]

Coming out of the All-Star break, Toronto continued to struggle. Then, on July 30th, something special happened. Facing the Oakland A's, Delabar retired all three batters in order in the bottom of the 8th on nine pitches. Protecting a 5-run lead, Delabar faced Adam Rosales first and got him to chase three pitches (two four-seams and a slider) high in the strike zone. Next up, using both the top and the bottom of the zone, he pitched Coco Crisp a four-seam, and back-to-back two-seams, for three strikes. Finally, continuing to show impressive command, he went back to the mix that had

---

228 Brendan Kennedy, "Blue Jays' Steve Delabar voted to MLB all-star game," *Toronto Star* (July 11, 2013): http://www.thestar.com/sports/bluejays/2013/07/11/blue_jays_ steve_delabar_voted_to_mlb_allstar_game.html. Retrieved on July 31, 2013.

beat Rosales, and tossed Chris Young two four-seams and a slider for the final strikeout. This time, he went inside on the second pitch, then got him swinging, chasing a pitch that was low and outside. Obviously, what makes this immaculate inning particularly noteworthy is the timing at which it occurred in Delabar's career. Otherwise, the inning, while it did contribute to a win for his club, would not change the fortune for the Blue Jays that season. The Blue Birds did blank the A's that day though, 5-0.

In addition to his immaculate inning, Delabar also made history for another rare accomplishment. On July 30th, 2012, he became the first pitcher in Major League history to strike out four men in extra innings.[229] Two weeks after he was traded from Seattle, Delabar struck out four batters in the 10th inning facing the Chicago White Sox. He became the first pitcher in Major League history to fan four in extra innings, after Tyler Flowers struck out but was allowed to advance to first on a passed ball. All told, Delabar struck out 6 batters that night in only 2 innings of work. The Jays would go on to beat the Sox, 3-2.

Through 2014, Delabar had a 13-9 record, 3.72 ERA, and 202 strikeouts. Although an All-Star in 2013, Delabar's 2014 season was a considerable letdown for the right-handed reliever. While starting the season with the Jays, a series of poor performances saw him demoted to Triple-A Buffalo.

Steve Delabar's Perfect Inning Pitch by Pitch[230]

Batter	Pitch Count	Pitch Type	Speed	Strike
	1	Fastball	94.0	Foul
Adam Rosales	2	Fastball	96.0	Swinging Strike
	3	Slider	86.9	Swinging Strike
	1	Fastball	95.0	Called Strike
Coco Crisp	2	Fastball	95.3	Swinging Strike
	3	Fastball	96.8	Swinging Strike
	1	Fastball	95.9	Called Strike
Chris Young	2	Fastball	95.7	Called Strike
	3	Slider	86.4	Swinging Strike

229 Robert MacLeod, "Delabar makes history in Blue Jay's walkoff win," *Globe and Mail* (Aug. 13, 2012): http://www.theglobeandmail.com/sports/delabar-makes-history-in-blue-jays-walkoff-win/article4479881/. Retrieved on December 16, 2014.

230 Brook's Baseball Pitchf/x: http://www.brooksbaseball.net/pfxVB. Retrieved on November 15, 2014.

Brad Boxberger
May 8th, 2014

Tampa Bay Rays pitcher Brad Boxberger was the sixty-seventh pitcher to pitch an immaculate inning in the history of the game, and the first of the 2014 season. 2014 proved to be a remarkable season for immaculate innings, with a record seven recorded. Born in Fullerton, California, on May 27th, 1988, the right-handed pitcher Boxberger attended the University of Southern California (USC), where he played baseball for the USC Trojans. Some readers may recall that one of the coaches for the USC Trojans, Tom House, figured prominently in the Disney film, *Million Dollar Arm,* a film about the first Indian pitchers to be signed by a Major League club (Rinku Singh and Dinesh Patel for the Pirates). House, played by Bill Paxton, is portrayed as an unconventional pitching coach, who uses psychology as much as mechanics for training purposes. Through these methods, he was able to coach Rinku and Dinesh to successful Major League tryouts. House has also worked with many notable NFL quarterbacks, such as Tom Brady, Drew Brees and Tim Tebow.[231] As he was the coach at USC at the time Boxberger was there, we can also add Brad to House's list of successful

---

231 Kenny Legan, "Pitching guru Tom House also tutors top NFL quarterbacks," NFL Network (July 25, 2012): http://www.nfl.com/news/story/09000d5d82acaf67/article/pitching-guru-tom-house-also-tutors-top-nfl-quarterbacks. Retrieved on November 18, 2014.

prospects. A right-handed pitcher, Boxberger was drafted in the first round (forty-third overall) of the 2009 draft by the Cincinnati Reds but was traded to the Padres in 2011. He made his first appearance on June 10th, 2012. In 2014, he was traded to the Rays.

According to scouting reports, Boxberger is best suited for set-up or closer roles in the bullpen. He has a fastball that typically clocks between 90 and 95 mph, a slider and a curve ball in the low to mid-80s and a change-up in the low to mid-70s.[232] Through to the end of the 2014 season, he had a 5-3 record, 2.61 ERA, and 161 strikeouts.

On May 8th, 2014, the Rays faced the Orioles at Tropicana Field. Those in attendance at the Trop (never big numbers regardless of how well the Rays are playing) got to witness a truly rare event. By the 6th inning, the Orioles were ahead by 2 runs. David Price, having given up a two-run homer in the second and an RBI single in the 4th, surrendered back-to-back singles and a walk in the top of the 6th, when Joe Maddon signaled for Boxberger. He proceeded to strike out the next three batters, leaving two runners stranded. First up, he struck out Steve Pearce, who chased a 96 mph high fastball for strike three. Number eight hitter, Jonathan Schoop was next, and he struck out swinging on a 95 mph fastball. Finally, Caleb Joseph, went down swinging at a 95 mph fastball. Boxberger faced another two batters in the top of the 7th before being replaced by Joel Peralta. Over 1.1 innings, he walked 1 batter with 3 strikeouts and no runs or hits allowed. However, the Rays were unable to close the gap and lost, 3-1.

Boxberger's immaculate inning bears some further comment. It is the only recorded instance of perfect inning that has occurred with a man already on base. As he came in relief, it is fair that he gets the record: after all, the first 3 batters he faced were retired on nine pitches. Moreover, the added stress of having two runners on with no-outs makes Boxberger's achievement just a little more impressive than most.

---

232 John Sickels, "Rookie Review: Brad Boxberger, RHP, San Diego Padres," Minor League Baseball (Sept. 26 2012): http://www.minorleagueball.com/2012/9/26/3415080/rookie-review-brad-boxberger-rhp-san-diego-padres. Retrieved on November 18, 2014.

Brad Boxberger's Perfect Inning Pitch by Pitch[233]

Batter	Pitch Count	Pitch Type	Speed	Strike
Steve Pearce	1	Change-up	80.0	Foul
	2	Change-up	80.0	Foul
	3	Fastball	95.7	Swinging Strike
Jonathan Schoop	1	Fastball	94.0	Called Strike
	2	Change-up	81.4	Foul
	3	Fastball	95.0	Swinging Strike
Caleb Joseph	1	Change-up	80.8	Called Strike
	2	Fastball	95.8	Foul
	3	Fastball	95.0	Swinging Strike

233 Brooks Baseball Pitchf/x: http://www.brooksbaseball.net/pfxVB. Retrieved on November 16, 2014.

Cole Hamels
May 17th, 2014

Colbert Michael "Cole" Hamels has played his entire Major League career as a starting pitcher for the Philadelphia Phillies. Drafted seventeenth overall in the first round (right out of high school) during the '02 draft, his first game in the Majors occurred on May 12th, 2006. A lefty, Hamels is known to possess one of the best change-ups in the game, which is described as "soft sinker that just falls down."[234] He also possesses a four-seam fastball that clocks in around 90-92 mph, along with a cutter in the high 80s.[235] A three-time All-Star (2007, 2011 and 2012), Hamels won both the National League Championship Series and World Series MVP Awards in 2008. On September 1st, 2014, he pitched a combined no-hitter against the Braves (Hamel was pulled in 7th inning). Through 2014, his career stats include a 108-83 record, 3.27 ERA, and 1,707 strikeouts.

The second immaculate inning of the 2014 season came in a May 17th rout against the Cincinnati Reds—a game the Phillies won, 12-1. After a rough two innings that luckily only resulted in 1 run, Hamels took the hill in the 3rd and retired the side on nine pitches. Facing the 2nd, 3rd and

---

234 Michael Bamberger, "Cole Hamels figures to be key in World Series," SI.com (Oct. 22, 2008): Retrieved on April 14, 2014.

235 "Cole Hamels," FanGraphs: http://www.fangraphs.com/statss.aspx?playerid=4972 &position=P. Retrieved on November 16, 2014.

4th batters in Reds lineup, all three went down swinging. Zack Cozart, faced a fastball-cutter-fastball volley, swinging for the third strike. Hamel then threw two 92-93 mph fastballs in a row at Brandon Phillips, before a third strike curve dismissed him. Finally, Todd Frazier swung through three pitches, a change-up and two more fastballs, for the final out of the inning. The Phillies broke out from there, chasing the starter and scoring 11 runs in total. Hamels notched the win. He pitched 7 innings allowing only 3 hits, 1 earned run, while walking 2 batters and striking out 10 on the day. While still early in the season, the Phillies were in fifth place after the win, with an overall record of 18-22. Reds' manager Byran Price had this to say about the opposing starter: "He's good. I know he's not off to a great start this year and he started on the DL, he's back. That's what our scouting reports said. He looks like the regular guy, good velocity, both sides of the plate. He's got all the accoutrements—he's got the cutter and the change and the curve ball and good fastball command. He pitched a good game. Hopefully we'll be able to challenge him a bit more the next time we see him."[236]

To my mind, Hamels will be forever linked to the role he played in arguably one of the best starting rotations in baseball history that included Roy "Doc" Halladay, Cliff Lee and Roy Oswalt. Doc, Lee and Hamels were all in the top five for Cy Young votes in 2011. As impressive as that unit was, and it should be remembered that Lee was out in 2010 then back again for 2011, the Phillies could not win the ultimate prize with this powerhouse starting core. Halladay retired in 2013, and Hamels suffered a number of injuries, undergoing surgeries for his elbow and a hernia.[237] In 2014, he missed Opening Day, owing to tendonitis in his biceps and did not play in a game until April 23rd.

Outside of baseball, Cole and his wife Heidi have a philanthropic project, the Hamels Foundation, which is dedicated to improving the lives of children through education. The project began in 2008 and currently supports programs in both Philly and in Africa.

---

236 C. Trent Rosecrans, "Bailey roughed up early as Reds fall to the Phillies," *Cincinnati Inquirer* (May 18, 2014): http://www.cincinnati.com/story/sports/mlb/reds/2014/05/17/reds-phillies/9235017/. Retrieved on November 16, 2014.

237 D.J. Short, "Cole Hamels undergoes elbow, hernia surgeries," HardBall Talk (Oct. 15, 2011): http://hardballtalk.nbcsports.com/2011/10/15/cole-hamels-undergo(es-elbow-hernia-surgeries/. Retrieved on November 16, 2014.

Cole Hamels' Perfect Inning Pitch by Pitch[238]

Batter	Pitch Count	Pitch Type	Speed	Strike
	1	Fastball	90.7	Called Strike
Zack Cozart	2	Cutter	89.4	Foul
	3	Fastball	92.3	Swinging Strike
	1	Fastball	92.0	Called Strike
Brandon Phillips	2	Fastball	93.3	Called Strike
	3	Curve	79.3	Swinging Strike
	1	Change-up	85.6	Swinging Strike
Todd Frazier	2	Fastball	94.0	Swinging Strike
	3	Fastball	94.5	Swinging Strike

238 Brooks Baseball Pitchf/x: http://www.brooksbaseball.net/pfxVB. Retrieved on November 16, 2014.

Justin Masterson
June 2nd, 2014

Justin Daniel Masterson is responsible for recording the seventy-fourth immaculate inning, and the third of the 2014 season. An American born in Jamaica on March 22nd, 1985, Masterson was drafted by the Red Sox in the second round of the 2006 draft, out of San Diego State University. His Major League debut came two years later, on April 24th. He began the 2014 season playing for the Cleveland Indians, but was traded to St. Louis on the 30th of July. In 2015, he signed back with the Red Sox. His career numbers to the end of 2014 include a 60-72 record, 4.24 ERA and 955 strikeouts.

While with Cleveland, Masterson made the 2013 American League All-Star Team. He led the league in putouts in 2010, and become one of only seventy-two players in Major League Baseball history to strike out four batters in a single inning (August 4th, 2011). He also holds the distinction of being the first Red Sox pitcher since the opening of Fenway Park in 1912 to win four consecutive starts at home. The last one, on June 8th 2008, he pitched in 98 degree heat, which didn't seem to phase him at all: "I love the heat, I don't think it can really get too hot for me to have too much fun out there."[239] He comes by his love for heat honestly, being the first Jamaican-born pitcher in the Majors.

---

239 Baxter Holmes, "Fun in games for Masterson. Rookie undefeated in first four starts," *Boston Globe* (June 9, 2008): http://www.boston.com/sports/baseball/redsox/articles/2008/06/09/fun_in_games_for_masterson/. Retrieved on August 15, 2014.

Masterson's pitching style has been compared to that of Dennis Eckersley's, owing to the three-quarter, sliding motion of his arm.[240] A righty, he has a number of pitches he can draw on, including a fastball that typically ranges in high 80s to low 90s. He also commands a sinker, change-up and slider.[241] The slider proved particularly effective in his perfect inning.

On June 2nd, 2014, in an evening game pitting Cleveland against the Red Sox, the third immaculate inning of the '14 season was pitched. Facing the 6th, 7th, and 8th hitters in the Red Sox line-up that night, Masterson took the mound in the top of the 4th, having struggled to find the zone in the previous three innings and having already thrown 62 pitches. Facing Jonny Gomes first, Masterson dispatched him quickly with a fastball-slider combination that resulted in a called strike and two chops at the air. The last two sliders were shockingly cruel, just dropping out of the zone and clearly fooling Gomes. Grady Sizemore came in next and haplessly swung through a slider for strike three. The final batter, Stephen Drew, missed arguably the most hittable pitch thrown by Masterson in that inning (93 mph fastball) but then swung at strike three for the ninth pitch of the inning that finished the side.

The Indians went on to win, 3-2. Masterson pitched 7 innings, allowing just 3 hits, 4 walks and no runs for the win. Masterson's success that evening was an examplar of his whole season, one in which he developed the ability to use his slider against lefties.[242] Prior to 2013, Masterson's strikeout rate against lefties was 13%. By 2013, it was close to 20%; however, his early season improvement may have been a blip, as by August of '14, lefties were hitting +.300 against him.

---

240 "Justin Masterson," Wikipedia: http://en.wikipedia.org/wiki/Justin_Masterson. Retrieved on January 4, 2015.

241 "Justin Masterson," FanGraphs: http://www.fangraphs.com/statss.aspx?playerid=2038 &position=P. Retrieved on January 4, 2015.

242 August Fagerstrom, "Justin Masterson's Immaculate Inning (And Then Some)," FanGraphs (June 4, 2014): http://www.fangraphs.com/blogs/justin-mastersons-immaculate-inning-and-then-some/. Retrieved on August 15, 2014.

Justin Masterson's Perfect Inning Pitch by Pitch[243]

Batter	Pitch Count	Pitch Type	Speed	Strike
	1	Fastball	91.6	Called Strike
Jonny Gomes	2	Slider	84.4	Swinging Strike
	3	Slider	82.9	Swinging Strike
	1	Sinker	90.2	Called Strike
Grady Sizemore	2	Fastball	92.2	Foul
	3	Slider	84.4	Swinging Strike
	1	Fastball	93.1	Called Strike
Stephen Drew	2	Slider	83.9	Called Strike
	3	Slider	83.5	Swinging Strike (Blocked)

243 Brooks Baseball Pitchf/x: http://www.brooksbaseball.net/pfxVB. Retrieved on November 30, 2014.

Garrett Richards
June 4th, 2014

The fourth immaculate inning of the '14 season occurred just two days after the third and was pitched by right-hander Garrett Richards of the Angels. Richards was born in Riverside, California, and made his Major League debut for the Angels on August 10th, 2011. He was drafted forty-second overall by the Angels in the '09 draft. Through to the end of 2014, he had a 24-17 record, 3.66 ERA, and 321 strikeouts. Richards has a number of options he can go to on the mound: two- and four-seam fastballs with running action (toping out in the 95-99 mph), change-ups to lefties, sliders to righties and a nasty curveball. Joe Girardi called Richards fastball "exceptional," owing to its movement.[244] In 2014, he was an American League All-Star Final Vote nominee. His most impressive record to date however was becoming part of the immaculate inning fraternity. He also has the distinction of having pitched his immaculate inning on the 125th anniversary of John Clarkson's perfect inning, the first one in the history of the game.

Richards took the mound in the bottom of the 2nd on June 4th, 2014, facing John Singleton, Matt Dominguez and Chris Carter of the Astros. Still scoreless, John Singleton began the inning by swinging at an 80 mph

---

244 Brooks Baseball PitchFX Tool - Player Card: Garrett Richards, Retrieved on August 10, 2014.

curveball for strike three. Dominguez was called out looking at strike three, on a bullet of a fastball clocking in at 97 mph. The same fate befell Carter, who swung on and missed an 86.6 mph slider for strike three. In nine pitches, these batters faced a mix of high 90 mph fastballs, sinkers and curves in perfect execution. Richards would pitch 8 innings that game, allowing only 4 hits, no walks and striking out 9 batters. The Angels took the game, 4-0. Richard's performance was in many ways a reaction to his previous outing in which he surrendered 5 runs on 5 hits and 3 walks in the first inning. Angels' catcher Hank Conger was asked about Richards after his immaculate performance and said: "He definitely pitched like he had a little chip on his shoulder. You could obviously tell he was antsy about the start. It was good for him to clear his mind and get back on the mound after his last outing. You could definitely see right off the get go it was coming out pretty hot. It was amazing tonight."[245]

Garrett Richard's Perfect Inning Pitch by Pitch

Batter	Pitch Count	Pitch Type	Speed	Strike
John Singleton	1	Sinker	97.2	Foul
	2	Slider	88.2	Swinging Strike
	3	Curve	80.0	Swinging Strike
Matt Dominguez	1	Fastball	96.8	Called Strike
	2	Sinker	97.5	Foul
	3	Fastball	97.4	Called Strike
Chris Carter	1	Fastball	97.8	Swinging Strike
	2	Curve	79.4	Swinging Strike
	3	Slider	88.6	Swinging Strike

245 "Astros draw blank against Angels, Richards" *Reuters* (June 05,2014): http://sports-news.us/2014/06/05/astros-draw-blank-against-angels-richards-reuters/. Retrieved on August 10, 2014.

Rex Brothers
June 14th, 2014

Just ten days after Richard's record, Rockies left-hander, Rex Coleman Brothers pitched the fifth immaculate inning of the year. The 2014 season may well be remembered for having three immaculate innings pitched in a twelve-day period in early June. Indeed, two more immaculate innings occurred in May, meaning five of the seven innings occurred in just over a month, early in the season. Brothers, born in Murfreesboro, Tennessee, debuted for the Rockies on June 6th, 2011. Prior to the Majors, he spent two seasons playing minor ball, and was the NCAA Freshman of the Year playing for Lipscomb University in 2007.

Brothers moved to the Closer role in 2013, when Rafael Betancourt was taken down by injuries. He took to the role admirably, as he recorded 19 saves in 21 chances. He posted a 1.74 ERA, including a run of 30 scoreless innings in just 32 games. Based on his performance, it seemed likely Brothers would get the nod as closer for the 2014 season, until the Rockies signed LaTroy Hawkins for $2.5 million in the off-season. As a righty, Hawkins gave the club options with Brothers in the wings to handle lefty match-ups. At least at the beginning of the 2014 campaign, Brothers seemed content with his role, "I have to be honest. I've always wanted to be a closer. I've worked toward it. But I will take on whatever my role entails. When we signed LaTroy, I was excited. I think we were looking for ways to make our ball club better."[246] Little did he know that just a few months later, he would make history.

In the bottom of the 8th on June 14th, 2014, Brothers took the mound to face Michael Morse, Brandon Crawford and Gregor Blanco. The Giants were ahead by a run, when Morse came to the plate. A 92 mph fastball on the third pitch left Morse looking. Crawford went down the same way, looking at 91.6 mph fastball. Blanco swung on the ninth pitch of the inning, an 87 mph slider. Looking at the Pitchf/x data, Brothers' velocity on those nine pitches showed good range, peaking at just over 92-mph (fastballs) and dipping at or just below 85-mph on sliders. Morse, for example, was offered a 90.5, 85.5 and 92.3 mph combination, enough variation in speed to play havoc with a batter's timing. More impressive was Brothers command of the zone. Four of the nine pitches were down in the zone while three others were down and away. The remaining two pitches, one in almost the middle of the zone and the other inside top corner, were both called strikes.

Following Brothers spectacular 8th, the Rockies scored 2 runs off an inside the park home run by Brandon Barnes. Brother's day was done but the Rockies took the game, 5-4. Brothers' thoughts on his 8th inning reflect a common theme of this book: immaculate innings can be easily missed even by the pitcher. "I came off the field and started thinking about the inning: 'That went pretty well, I guess. Not much thought came into my mind about it, but Mr. LaTroy Hawkins, he let me know when I got to the dugout," Brothers recalled.[247] His manager, Walt Weiss, later had more compliments "that was a huge performance for him today."[248] Weiss went on to say he knew the achievement was rare, accurately citing the number of times it has been done, and adding that he was pretty sure he had never seen it done before in person. Brothers' immaculate inning was also special because it was the first by a Rockies pitcher and the first at AT&T Park.

---

246 Patrick Saunders, "Any role in Rockies' bullpen is all right with lefty Rex Brothers," *The Denver Post* (Feb. 02, 2014): http://www.denverpost.com/rockies/ci_25159284/any-role-rockies-bullpen-is-all-right-lefty. Retrieved on August 2, 2014.

247 Anthony Rieber, "Three strikeouts on nine pitches? Whoa Brothers," *Newsday* (June 21, 2014): http://www.newsday.com/sports/columnists/anthony-rieber/three-strikeouts-on-nine-pitches-whoa-brothers-1.8527204. Retrieved on August 2, 2014.

248 Paul Casella, "Brothers tosses season's fifth immaculate inning," MLB.com (June 14, 2014): http://m.mlb.com/news/article/79811112/rockies-reliever-rex-brothers-pitches-seasons-fifth-immaculate-inning. Retrieved on August 2, 2014.

The latter is particularly remarkable given that AT&T Park, at one mile above sea level, is not known to be pitcher-friendly. At the end of the 2014 season, Brothers finished with a 15-11 record, 3.49 ERA, 273 strikeouts, and 20 saves.

Rex's Brothers Perfect Inning Pitch by Pitch

Batter	Pitch Count	Pitch Type	Speed	Strike
Michael Morse	1	Fastball	90.5	Called Strike
	2	Slider	85.5	Foul
	3	Fastball	92.3	Called Strike
Brandon Crawford	1	Slider	85.1	Swinging Strike
	2	Slider	85.2	Foul
	3	Fastball	91.6	Called Strike
Gregor Blanco	1	Fastball	90.6	Called Strike
	2	Slider	83.8	Called Strike
	3	Slider	86.7	Swinging Strike

Carlos Contreras
July 11th, 2014

The sixth pitcher to record an immaculate inning in the 2014 season was Carlos Manuel Contreras. Contreras' effort could be called the inning that nearly got away, as it was barely mentioned in popular media at the time. The fact that it was almost completely missed may be related to the fact that Contreras, outside of Cincinnati, is a relatively unknown pitcher. Born on January 8th, 1991, in Santo Domingo, Dominican Republic, Contreras was signed as an amateur free agent in 2008 by the Reds. After the 2012 season, he was added to the 40-man roster and named to the All-Star Futures Game in 2013. Contreras made his debut on June 21st, 2014, in a game against the Blue Jays. A right-handed pitcher, Contreras relies mostly on his fastball (77% in 2014), curve ball (13%) and change-up (10%); however, the sample size of his stuff in the Majors is very small. At the end of the 2014 season, he had a 0-1 record, 6.52 ERA, and 19 strikeouts.

Though largely unknown, Contreras made baseball history by becoming the seventy-second pitcher to retire the side on nine pitches. The game in question occurred against the Pittsburgh Pirates at Great American Ball Park on July 11th, 2014. After surrendering a run in the 6th, Contreras returned in the 7th and was immaculate. Facing Jordy Mercer, Jeff Locke, and Gregory Polanco, Contreras dispatched the side quickly. A fastball-change-up-fastball combination felled Mercer, who swung through strike three. Locke, had three called strikes, all perfectly placed in the bottom of the zone—an 82 mph curve was called for strike three. Finally, Polanco was the only hitter in that half of the inning to catch a piece of Contreras' fastball. Back-to-back change-ups, both of which were low, resulted in two swinging strikes. For Contreras, that would be it for the day. He left the game having pitched 2 innings, allowing 1 run off 2 hits, walking 2 batters and recording 4 strikeouts. Perhaps inspired by Contreras' perfect inning, the Reds would begin to chip away at the Pirates' 4-run lead. In the 7th inning, they scored 2 runs, and then 3 more in the 8th to take a 1-run lead. The Pirates could not get a run in the bottom of the 9th, and the Reds claimed the win, 6-5.

Other than his perfect inning, Contreras' numbers for his first season in the big leagues are anything but impressive. Only time will tell whether he will be remembered for anything beyond his immaculate 7th inning performance against Pittsburgh.

Carlos Contreras' Perfect Inning Pitch by Pitch[249]

Batter	Pitch Count	Pitch Type	Speed	Strike
	1	Fastball	92.0	Called Strike
Jordy Mercer	2	Change-up	84.1	Swinging Strike
	3	Fastball	95.7	Swinging Strike
	1	Fastball	92.0	Called Strike
Jeff Locke	2	Fastball	93.5	Called Strike
	3	Curve	82.0	Called Strike
	1	Fastball	92.4	Fouled
Gregory Polanco	2	Change-up	87.0	Swinging Strike
	3	Change-up	89.7	Swinging Strike

---

249 Brooks Baseball Pitchf/x: http://www.brooksbaseball.net/pfxVB. Retrieved on November 4, 2014.

Brandon McCarthy
September 17th, 2014

The last pitcher up to the end of the 2014 season to pitch a perfect inning is Brandon McCarthy. A starting right-hander, McCarthy was born on July 7th, 1983, in Glendale, California. He attended Cheyenne Mountain High School in Colorado Springs and Lamar Community College. McCarthy was drafted by the Chicago White Sox during the seventeenth round of the 2002 amateur draft. His very first appearance in the Major Leagues was with Chicago on May 22nd, 2005 against the cross-town rival Cubs. That year, the White Sox would go to the World Series, but McCarthy did not pitch in the postseason. McCarthy has played with six clubs in his career so far: the White Sox (2005-06), Rangers (2007-09), Athletics (2011-12), Diamondbacks (2013-14), Yankees (2014) and Dodgers (2015). At end of the 2014 season, he had a 52-65 record, 4.09 ERA, and 698 strikeouts.

When McCarthy began his career, he relied mainly on four pitches: fastball, slider, curveball and change-up. However, by 2011 he had replaced his curveball with a cutter and added a split-fingered fastball to the mix.[250]

A dramatic chapter in McCarthy's career came in 2012 when he was struck on the head by a line drive up the middle. McCarthy had begun

---

250 "Brandon McCarthy" Fangraphs: http://www.fangraphs.com/statss.aspx?playerid=4662 &position=P#pitchtype. Retrieved November 4, 2014.

the 2012 season in fine form, even pitching the season opener for the A's. However, on September 5, 2012, there was a moment when everyone feared the worst. In a game against the Angels, McCarthy was struck on the back of the head by a line drive off the bat of Erick Aybar. The images were scary: McCarthy lay on the ground after the hit, but managed to lift himself to a sitting position. While he was able to leave the field under his own power, a CT scan later showed signs of an epidural hemorrhage and skull fracture. McCarthy underwent a two-hour surgery to relieve pressure that had built up from the bleeding. Fortunately, the surgery and his recovery were both successful, and while he would not play for the rest of the season, he was well enough to cheer on his teammates in the dugout for the postseason.

On September 17th, 2014, pitching for the Yankees, amidst the extended farewell tour of captain Derek Jeter, McCarthy took the mound to face the Tampa Bay Rays. By that point in September, any hope for postseason play had been all but extinguished for the club. Starting the game, McCarthy came out in the 7th to face the 5th, 6th and 7th batters of the Rays. Protecting a 1-run lead, McCarthy retired Wil Myers with a curveball-sinker-fastball combination. Myers looked at an 80-mph curve, fouled of off an 92 mph sinker and finally swung through a 94 mph fastball. Next up, Nick Franklin swung through a 91.6 mph cutter for strike one, fouled off an 80 mph curve and then swung through a 94.6 mph fastball for strike three. Finally, Matt Joyce swung through an 81 mph curveball, fouled off a cutter clocking in at over 92 mph, then left the plate swinging on a 94.6 mph cutter. McCarthy earned the win in a 3-2 game, pitching 7 innings while allowing just 2 earned runs on 4 hits. His wife, upon learning of his immaculate feat, tweeted: "Immaculate inning. I think I just found the name for my new band."[251]

The final pitcher in this collection not only earned the seventy-third spot on the all-time list, his immaculate inning broke another record: seven perfect innings by seven different pitchers in the same season.

251 Joe Lemire, "Brandon McCarthy Breaks Down His 'Immaculate Inning," *Wall Street Journal* (Sept. 18, 2014): http://online.wsj.com/articles/yankees-pitcher-catcher-break-down-immaculate-inning-against-tampa-bay-1411087960. Retrieved on November 4, 2014.

Brandon McCarthy's Perfect Inning Pitch by Pitch[252]

Batter	Pitch Count	Pitch Type	Speed	Strike
	1	Curve	80.4	Called Strike
Wil Myers	2	Sinker	92.0	Fouled Off
	3	Fastball	94.3	Swinging Strike
	1	Cutter	91.6	Swinging Strike
Nick Franklin	2	Curve	80.4	Fouled Off
	3	Fastball	94.6	Swinging Strike
	1	Curve	81.4	Swinging Strike
Matt Joyce	2	Cutter	92.1	Fouled
	3	Cutter	94.6	Swinging Strike

---

252 Brooks Baseball Pitchf/x: http://www.brooksbaseball.net/pfxVB. Retrieved on November 4, 2014.

EPILOGUE

Up to this point, the focus of this book has been on pitchers: a reasonable thing given that a perfect inning is about pitching excellence. Yet, the complete story is really about the duel between the hurler and the batter (not to mention the catcher who is making the calls). So the story would be incomplete if we did not at least take a closer look at the other players in this contest and what the history of perfect innings looks like from more of a team perspective. To do this though, I am going to shift from narratives back to numbers. Here are two specific considerations that stand out when you examine the history of perfect innings.

Number of hitters who have been victimized more than once

A total of 231 batters have been struck out in the course of an immaculate inning over the history of the event. How many of these batters were the victims of a perfect inning more than once? The answer is ten: Larry Herndon (San Francisco Giants both times), Carlton Fisk (Boston Red Sox first time, White Sox the second), Greg Luzinski (Phillies the first time, White Sox the second), Eric Anthony (Houston Astros first time, Seattle Mariners second), Jeff Reed (Reds first time, Colorado Rockies second), Ellis Burks (Rockies both times), Jose Vizcaino (Astros both times), Juan Encarnación (Tigers first time, Marlins second), Khalil Greene (Padres first time, Cardinals second), and Julio Lugo (Astros first time, Cardinals second). No player in history so far has been victimized more than twice. Just to pile some more statistics onto this point, 73 different pitchers have pitched a perfect inning, but only four have done so more than once. That is 5.5% of all immaculate inning pitchers, while the proportion of batters who have been in more than one immaculate inning is 4.4%. Clearly, being part of more than one immaculate inning, regardless of whether you are pitcher or a hitter, is a very rare occurrence in an already very rare event. That in and of itself is a noteworthy addition to the annals of baseball history.

Immaculate innings by team

Other questions that arise are directed at teams as a whole—how many teams have had pitchers pitch an immaculate inning? Are there any teams that have never had a pitcher accomplish this feat? Table 2 shows the number of immaculate innings pitched by teams that are still in existence today (but may have been in different cities or had different names in the past making this kind of analysis very tricky indeed). To address this complexity, I need to take some liberties. For example, for the Dodgers, I combined results for Brooklyn and Los Angeles into a single group. I did the same for the Athletics, combining Philadelphia, Kansas City and Oakland together (even though no immaculate innings were pitched against KC). Because Houston changed its name from the Colt .45s to the Astros in 1965, I also combined their results into a single franchise. Because the Atlanta Braves organization can be traced back to the Boston and Milwaukee I have included the former with the latter two. I have, however, excluded the Boston Beaneaters from consideration altogether, as they are of historical interest only as no direct ties to any club today can be traced.

Table 1. Teams by number of immaculate innings they have recorded

0	1	2	3	4+
Minnesota Twins	Colorado Rockies	Boston Red Sox	Milwaukee Brewers	Arizona Diamondbacks
Texas Rangers	Cleveland Indians	Toronto Blue Jays	Baltimore Orioles	Chicago Cubs
		San Francisco/ New York Giants	Kansas City Royals	New York Yankees
	Seattle Mariners	Pittsburgh Pirates	Boston/ Milwaukee/ Atlanta Braves	Houston Colt .45s / Astros
		Cincinnati Reds		Philadelphia Phillies

0	1	2	3	4+
San Diego Padres	St. Louis Cardinals			Brooklyn/LA Dodgers
Miami / Florida Marlins	New York Mets			Philadelphia / KC /Oakland A's
Chicago White Sox	Detroit Tigers			Washington Nationals*
	LA/California/ Anaheim Angels			

*Montreal Expos (3)

Of all the teams in existence in the league today, only the Twins and Rangers have never had a pitcher pitch an immaculate inning. At the opposite end of the spectrum, eight clubs—the Diamondbacks, Cubs, Yankees, Astros (Colt .45s), Phillies, A's, Nationals and Dodgers have recorded four or more immaculate innings (after we take into account that some of these clubs have played in more than one city). Remember of course, of the five times the Dodgers have recorded a perfect inning, three of them happened when Koufax was on the mound. Similarly, three of the four immaculate innings credited to the A's happened when that club was in Philadelphia— two from Lefty Grove and one from the Rube Waddell—two more of the greatest pitchers in the history of the game. Finally, I have included the Nationals in this grouping but with an asterisk: three of the four perfect innings happened when the team was in Montreal. Since moving to Washington, only one pitcher has achieved the same feat for the relocated club (Expos fans will surely take this as yet another sign the club should have never moved!). Two clubs, the Houston Colt .45s/Astros and the Yankees have the most recorded immaculate innings at six a piece. Given the disparity in club success between these last two franchises, they are indeed strange bedfellows when viewed in this light. Most of the remaining clubs still in existence today have had at least one recorded instance of an immaculate inning. The Brewers, Royals, and Braves (Boston/Atlanta) all have had three. What does this tell us if anything about the occurrence of an immaculate inning? Considering it has only occurred 76 times so far in the history of the game, it is fairly consistently spread across the majority of teams (at least those in the modern era). I say this because if we consider the fact that most of the immaculate innings pitched have occurred after 1960 (66 of 78 or 85%), the period where expansion of leagues began, then we can estimate after the fact how many of these teams should have been able to claim an immaculate inning pitched, if pitching one was evenly distributed across teams. I arrive at this conclusion by somewhat creative mathematical gymnastics. If we divide the number of immaculate innings that occurred from 1960 to 2014, which is 67, by the average number of teams in the league during this period (this is where it gets a little tricky owing to on-going expansions during this period but let's say 25, which takes into account there were 20 teams in 1962, but 30 by 1998) [253], then if immaculate innings were in fact evenly distributed, we would expect about 2.7 immaculate innings per club. Looking at Table 2, the numbers are actually not that far off. A total of 21 clubs have at least two immaculate innings credited to them.

If we look at this the other way round and ask how many teams have had immaculate innings pitched against them, the results look a bit different (see Table 3). I used the same groupings as before except this time I lumped the Philadelphia Quakers (1889) with the club they eventually became—the Phillies. There are a couple of noticeable differences when the tables are compared. First, there are now four teams under the zero column (instead of two), one of whom is the New York Yankees, who have not yet had an immaculate inning committed against them. There are also more clubs in the four or more column than before: the Phillies take top prize having had a total of seven immaculate innings pitched against them. The next most victimized clubs are the Houston Colt .45's/Astros and the Boston/Milwaukee/Atlanta Braves, both with five. Houston holds the dubious distinction of being one of the clubs with the most immaculate innings pitched for *and* the most pitched against. What is also apparent when looking at the chronology of occurrences of teams who were batting during an immaculate inning is the number of consecutive times a single team has been on the receiving end of a perfect inning. For example, all three of the immaculate innings pitched in 1979 occurred when the San

---

253 I came up with this estimate based on the following: By 1962, there were 20 teams, 10 in each League. By 1998, the number of teams was 30. If we simply average the two numbers, we get 25. While it is a somewhat coarse approach, it is not completely unreasonable. If we take the upper and lower number of teams instead, our estimates would range from 2.2 to 3.35. Of course, there was also a lot of relocation happening in this period. The consideration here is on expansion because at a club level, it does not really matter if the team has relocated. I do concede there are more complicated ways of approaching this analysis.

Francisco Giants were the opposing team. The Giants finished in fourth place that season in the NL West, with a 71 and 91 record. While far from a winning season, they were not the worst team in the majors that year: The Blue Jays won less than a third of their regular season games that year, finishing with a 53 and 109 record. Moreover, consecutive immaculate innings by the same team have occurred six times since 1925: White Sox (1925, 1953), Dodgers (1968, 1969), Phillies (both in the same season, 1971), Braves (again, both in the same season, 1998) and Marlins (same as the previous two, both occurrence in 2008).

Table 2. Teams by the number of times an immaculate inning was pitched against them

0	1	2	3	4+
Blue Jays	Detroit Tigers	Chicago Cubs	New York Mets	Boston/ Milwaukee/ Atlanta Braves
Minnesota Twins	Kansas City Royals	California/Anaheim/ LA Angels	St. Louis Cardinals	Chicago White Sox
Arizona Diamondbacks	Milwaukee Brewers	San Diego Padres	Cleveland Indians	Cincinnati Reds
New York Yankees	Texas Rangers	Pittsburgh Pirates	Colorado Rockies	Houston Colt .45s/Astros
	Montreal Expos/ Nationals	Philadelphia / KC /Oakland A's		Philadelphia Phillies
		Seattle Mariners		Brooklyn/LA Dodgers
		Tampa Bay Rays		New York/San Francisco Giants
				Baltimore Orioles
				Miami/Florida Marlins
				Boston Red Sox
		LA/California/ Anaheim Angels		

The fact that only a small number of batters have been on the receiving end of more than one immaculate inning, or that only a few teams have been on the opposing side in games were perfect innings have occurred more than once, is extremely curious. These facts, however, do not shed any additional light on why immaculate innings occur, or why they are increasing. Rather, I include them simply because they are interesting in their own right.

What might the future hold?

Extended instances of perfection in pitching, or other immaculate innings that have yet to occur, are almost as fascinating as what has actually happened in the game. For example, we have yet to have a recorded instance of more than one immaculate inning within the same game. While there have been numerous instances of four strike out innings in baseball, no pitcher to date has struck four batters out on just twelve pitches in a single inning. Although an immaculate inning has been pitched during the World Series (see Danny Jackson)—an immaculate inning has yet to occur in a clutch situation in the playoffs (e.g., retiring the side on nine pitches in the final inning of a decisive game). After watching Madison Baumgartner's performance in the 2014 World Series, I would bet on him being a good candidate to be the first to do so. As noted in the previous section, no player has batted in more than two immaculate innings.

Will the Jays, Yankees, Diamondbacks and Twins ever have their side retired on just nine pitches? Will the Twins ever have a pitcher who pitches a perfect inning? In 2014, there were more immaculate innings pitched in a single season than ever before in the game. Will the 2015 season see a new record? Or are we about to embark on another long, dry spell, like the one between the last recorded immaculate inning in the 1920s and the next one in 1953? Surely part of the mystique of baseball, indeed all sports, is the potential that what has been done before may never occur again. Unlike other sports though, baseball is more mysterious. It is not a game driven or dictated by time, like football or basketball. It defies time: an inning can take minutes or hours; a game, theoretically at least, may never end. With such uncertainties an inherent part of the game, one can be seduced into believing the past need not be prologue. At the same time, history shows us repeatedly the opposite is true. I have no doubt we will see other immaculate innings in the game. Waiting for the next perfect inning is one of the many things that keeps us coming back out to the park.

INDEX